S0-BNT-227

Subtracting Two-Digit Numbers

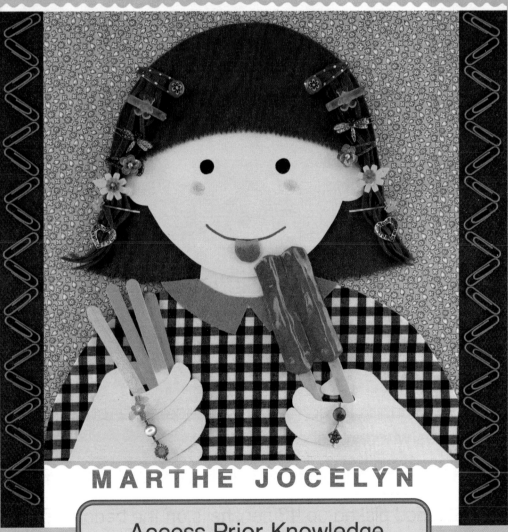

From the Read-Aloud Anthology

HANNAH'S Collections

MARTHE JOCELYN

Access Prior Knowledge

This story will help you review

- Modeling two-digit numbers
- Basic facts
- Adding two-digit numbers

Hannah loved to collect things. She found new treasures wherever she went.

Hannah found things with their own patterns from nature.

She had picked up 43 seashells on the beach last summer, and each had a different design. So did the shell of her pet turtle, Davey.

Hannah's 19 feathers had spots and speckles and stripes. Her 10 leaves had crisscrosses and curves and points.

Hannah chose barrettes with matching designs for Ellie. She could never decide if she had 14 barrettes or 7 pairs of barrettes. But when she and Ellie got dressed up, they looked very fancy indeed.

Altogether, Hannah had two dozen little creatures. She let Ellie look after the elephant family, who lived in the chocolate box. The others stood in a row along her shelf, lined up from the tallest to the smallest.

Hannah also collected jewelry. She had 5 rings. Sometimes she wore all of them on one hand. Or she might wear 4 on one hand and 1 on the other. Or 3 on one hand and 2 on the other.

Name_____

Use the story on pages 3l7b and 3l7c.
Use Workmat 3 and ▭▭▭▭▭ and ▫.
Solve.

Draw or write to explain.

1. Model the number of feathers.
   Model the number of leaves.
   Did she have more feathers or
   leaves? How many more?

   _____

   _____ more

2. Write two number sentences that
   tell how Hannah wore her rings.

   ____ + ____ = ____

   ____ + ____ = ____

3. Model the number of shells that
   Hannah picked up on the beach.

   If Hannah finds 3 more shells,
   how many will she have?

   _____ shells

4. **Create Your Own** Look at the picture on page 3l7b.
   Write a story about some of the items you see. Find the
   answer.

   _____

   _____

   _____

Dear Family,

My class is starting Unit 5. I will be learning about subtracting two-digit numbers with and without regrouping. These pages show some of what I will learn and have activities for us to do together.

From, _____

Vocabulary

These are some words I will use in this unit.

difference The answer to a subtraction problem

$$15 - 10 = 5 \qquad \begin{array}{r} 15 \\ -10 \\ \hline 5 \end{array}$$

difference └──→ 5

estimate An estimate is an answer that is close to an exact answer.

$$\begin{array}{r} 29 \\ -21 \end{array} \xrightarrow[\text{nearest ten}]{\text{round to}} \begin{array}{r} 30 \\ -20 \\ \hline 10 \end{array} \text{ estimate}$$

regroup In subtraction, to trade 1 ten for 10 ones (This used to be called "borrowing.")

1 ten = 10 ones

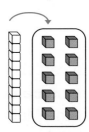

round To find which number another number is closer to

54 is closer to 50 than 60.
Round down. 54 rounds to 50.

50 51 52 53 54 55 56 57 58 59 60

Vocabulary Activity

Let's work together to complete these sentences.

1. In 15 − 8 = 7, the number 7 is the _____.

2. Sometimes when you subtract you need to _____ 1 ten as 10 ones.

Turn the page for more.

How To subtract two-digit numbers

This two-digit subtraction problem is an example of what I will be learning. Sometimes I will use tens and ones blocks to help me find the answer.

Subtract 32 − 18.

Step 1
Show 32. You need to subtract 8 ones.

Workmat 3	
Tens	Ones

Tens	Ones
3	2
− 1	8

Step 2
Regroup 1 ten as 10 ones.

Workmat 3	
Tens	Ones

Tens	Ones
2	12
3	2
− 1	8

Step 3
Subtract the ones.

Workmat 3	
Tens	Ones

Tens	Ones
2	12
3	2
− 1	8
	4

Step 4
Subtract the tens.

Workmat 3	
Tens	Ones

Tens	Ones
2	12
3	2
− 1	8
1	4

Literature

These books link to the math in this unit. We can look for them at the library.

A Remainder of One
by Elinor J. Pinczes
Illustrated by Bonnie MacKain
(Houghton Mifflin, 1995)

Math Curse
by Jon Scieszka

Let's read together!

Technology

We can visit *Education Place* at **eduplace.com/parents/mw/** for the Math Lingo game, the *e*•Glossary, and more games and activities to do together.

Regrouping With Subtraction

CHAPTER 12

INVESTIGATION

What subtraction problems can you make from this picture?

Stories About Stuff

Fill in the blanks to make your
own word story.
Draw a picture to show it.

Dora and her brother collect things.

She has 14 purple _____

and 8 red _____ in a shoebox.

Dora has _____ more purple items

than red items.

Marco collects 16 _____.

9 of the _____ are big. The rest of the _____ are

small. There are _____ more big items than small items.

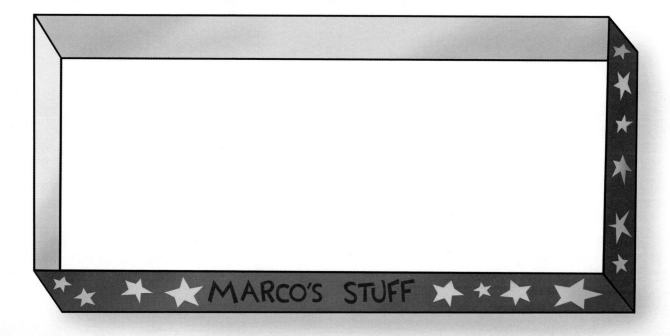

Name _____

Mental Math: Subtract Tens

Objective
Use mental math and basic facts to subtract tens.

Vocabulary
subtract
difference

When you **subtract** tens, think of a subtraction fact.

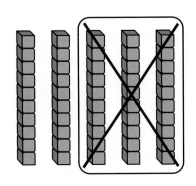

Find $50 - 30$.

$5 - 3 = \underline{\quad 2 \quad}$

5 tens $- 3$ tens $= \underline{\quad 2 \quad}$ tens

$50 - 30 = \underline{\quad 20 \quad}$

↑
difference

Guided Practice

Complete the subtraction sentences.
Use a basic fact to help.

1. Find $80 - 40$.

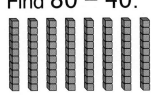

Think
$8 - 4$ helps me subtract the tens.

$8 - 4 = \underline{\qquad}$

8 tens $- 4$ tens $= \underline{\qquad}$ tens

$80 - 40 = \underline{\qquad}$

2. Find $60 - 30$.

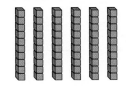

$6 - 3 = \underline{\qquad}$

6 tens $- 3$ tens $= \underline{\qquad}$ tens

$60 - 30 = \underline{\qquad}$

3. 5 tens $- 1$ ten $= \underline{\qquad}$ tens

$\underline{\qquad} - \underline{\qquad} = \underline{\qquad}$

4. 7 tens $- 2$ tens $= \underline{\qquad}$ tens

$\underline{\qquad} - \underline{\qquad} = \underline{\qquad}$

TEST TIPS **Explain Your Thinking** How does $7 - 2$ help you find $70 - 20$?

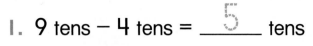

Remember to think about subtraction facts.

Complete the subtraction sentences.
Use a basic fact to help.

1. 9 tens − 4 tens = __5__ tens

   __90__ − __40__ = __50__

2. 4 tens − 2 tens = _____ tens

   _____ − _____ = _____

3. 9 tens − 7 tens = _____ tens

   _____ − _____ = _____

4. 3 tens − 1 ten = _____ tens

   _____ − _____ = _____

5. 8 tens − 3 tens = _____ tens

   _____ − _____ = _____

6. 5 tens − 2 tens = _____ tens

   _____ − _____ = _____

7. 3 tens − 2 tens = _____ ten

   _____ − _____ = _____

8. 7 tens − 3 tens = _____ tens

   _____ − _____ = _____

9. 8 tens − 1 ten = _____ tens

   _____ − _____ = _____

10. 9 tens − 3 tens = _____ tens

    _____ − _____ = _____

Problem Solving ▶ Reasoning

11. Pencils come in boxes of 10. Sandra has 6 boxes. She gives 4 boxes away. How many pencils does she have now?

Draw or write to explain.

_____ pencils

 At Home Give your child up to 9 dimes. Together create subtraction sentences. For example, 8 dimes − 3 dimes = 5 dimes.

Name _____

Subtract Tens on a Hundred Chart

MathTracks 2/1
Listen and Understand

Objective
Use a hundred chart and count back by tens to subtract.

Use the hundred chart.
Find 57 − 30.

 Step 1

Find 57 on the hundred chart.

1	2	3	4	5	6	7	8	9	10
11	12	13	14	15	16	17	18	19	20
21	22	23	24	25	26	27	28	29	30
31	32	33	34	35	36	37	38	39	40
41	42	43	44	45	46	47	48	49	50
51	52	53	54	55	56	57	58	59	60
61	62	63	64	65	66	67	68	69	70
71	72	73	74	75	76	77	78	79	80
81	82	83	84	85	86	87	88	89	90
91	92	93	94	95	96	97	98	99	100

Step 2

Move up 3 rows to subtract 30.

57 , 47, 37, 27

57 − 30 = __27__

Guided Practice

Use the hundred chart.
Subtract.

Think
Find 89.
Move up 2 rows.

1. 89 − 20 = ____
2. 35 − 10 = ____
3. 77 − 40 = ____
4. 95 − 30 = ____
5. 43 − 30 = ____
6. 70 − 60 = ____
7. 88 − 20 = ____
8. 64 − 50 = ____

9. 39
  −20

10. 62
  −50

11. 56
  −50

12. 93
  −50

13. 58
  −40

TEST TIPS **Explain Your Thinking** Look at 61, 51, 41, and 31 on the hundred chart. Describe the pattern. What number comes next?

Practice

Remember to move up 1 row for each ten you subtract.

Use the hundred chart.
Subtract.

1	2	3	4	5	6	7	8	9	10
11	12	13	14	15	16	17	18	19	20
21	22	23	24	25	26	27	28	29	30
31	32	33	34	35	36	37	38	39	40
41	42	43	44	45	46	47	48	49	50
51	52	53	54	55	56	57	58	59	60
61	62	63	64	65	66	67	68	69	70
71	72	73	74	75	76	77	78	79	80
81	82	83	84	85	86	87	88	89	90
91	92	93	94	95	96	97	98	99	100

1. 31 − 10 = __21__

2. 65 − 40 = _____

3. 74 − 30 = _____

4. 89 − 70 = _____

5. 55 − 20 = _____

6. 29 − 10 = _____

7. 44
   −20

8. 67
   −40

9. 92
   −60

10. 17
    −10

11. 90
    −80

12. 63
    −40

13. 31
    −20

14. 86
    −50

15. 79
    −30

16. 45
    −10

Algebra Readiness ▶ Number Sentences

17. Circle the number sentence that is not correct. Why is it wrong?

   59 + 20 = 79   59 − 20 = 39

   20 + 59 = 79   20 − 59 = 39

Draw or write to explain.

At Home Ask your child to show you how to find 94 − 50 on the hundred chart.

Name_____

Regroup Tens

 MathTracks 2/2
Listen and Understand

You can **regroup** 1 ten as 10 ones
to show a number another way.

Objective
Understand numbers
with and without
regrouping.
Vocabulary
regroup

Step 1

Here is one way to
show 34.

Workmat 3	
Tens	**Ones**
|||	▫▫▫▫

3 tens 4 ones = 34

Step 2

Regroup 1 ten as 10
ones.

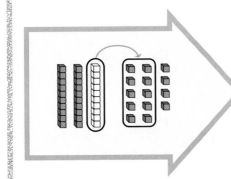

Step 3

Here is another way to
show 34.

Workmat 3	
Tens	**Ones**
||	▫▫▫▫▫▫▫▫▫▫▫▫▫▫

2 tens 14 ones = 34

Guided Practice

Use Workmat 3 with and .
Regroup 1 ten.
Write the tens and ones.

Think
I can show 53 a different
way when I regroup 1 of
the tens as 10 ones.

1. [53]   5 tens 3 ones   Regroup ⟩   _____ tens _____ ones

2. [46]   4 tens 6 ones   Regroup ⟩   _____ tens _____ ones

3. [29]   2 tens 9 ones   Regroup ⟩   _____ ten _____ ones

4. [64]   6 tens 4 ones   Regroup ⟩   _____ tens _____ ones

TEST TIPS **Explain Your Thinking** Describe what it means to regroup 1 ten.

Remember to regroup 1 ten as 10 ones.

Use Workmat 3 with ⬛⬛⬛⬛⬛⬛⬛⬛⬛⬛ and ⬛.
Regroup 1 ten. Write the tens and ones.

1. 62   6 tens 2 ones   Regroup ⟩   _____ tens _____ ones

2. 49   4 tens 9 ones   Regroup ⟩   _____ tens _____ ones

3. 32   3 tens 2 ones   Regroup ⟩   _____ tens _____ ones

4. 90   9 tens 0 ones   Regroup ⟩   _____ tens _____ ones

5. 54   5 tens 4 ones   Regroup ⟩   _____ tens _____ ones

6. 81   8 tens 1 one   Regroup ⟩   _____ tens _____ ones

7. 75   7 tens 5 ones   Regroup ⟩   _____ tens _____ ones

8. 96   9 tens 6 ones   Regroup ⟩   _____ ten _____ ones

Problem Solving ▶ Number Sense

Bill showed 37 this way.

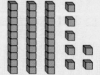

Jill showed 37 this way.

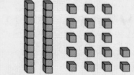

9. **Talk About It** Both are correct. Explain why.

At Home Ask your child to show the number 45 two different ways. Have him or her explain each way.

Decide When to Regroup

MathTracks 2/3
Listen and Understand

Objective
Decide when to regroup 1 ten as 10 ones to subtract.

Find 24 − 5.

Step 1

Show 2 tens and 4 ones. There are not enough ones to subtract 5.

Workmat 3	
Tens	Ones

Step 2

Regroup 1 ten as 10 ones.

Workmat 3	
Tens	Ones

Step 3

Subtract the ones. Write the difference.

Workmat 3	
Tens	Ones

1 ten 9 ones
19

Guided Practice

Use Workmat 3 with ⬛⬛⬛⬛⬛⬛⬛⬛⬛⬛ and ▣.

	Show the greater number.	Do you need to regroup to subtract?	Subtract the ones. How many tens and ones are left?		What is the difference?
1.	42 − 7	Yes No	__3__ tens	__5__ ones	35
2.	54 − 9	Yes No	_____ tens	_____ ones	
3.	36 − 2	Yes No	_____ tens	_____ ones	

TEST TIPS **Explain Your Thinking** How do you know when you need to regroup?

Chapter 12 Lesson 4

three hundred twenty-nine **329**

Practice

Remember to regroup when you need more ones to subtract.

Use Workmat 3 with ▱▱▱▱▱▱ and ▱.

	Show the greater number.	Do you need to regroup to subtract?	Subtract the ones. How many tens and ones are left?	What is the difference?
1.	56 – 7	(Yes) No	___4___ tens ___9___ ones	49
2.	43 – 8	Yes No	_____ tens _____ ones	
3.	37 – 7	Yes No	_____ tens _____ ones	
4.	65 – 3	Yes No	_____ tens _____ ones	
5.	24 – 7	Yes No	_____ ten _____ ones	
6.	72 – 9	Yes No	_____ tens _____ ones	
7.	98 – 5	Yes No	_____ tens _____ ones	

Problem Solving ▶ Number Sense

8. Henri has 28 stamps. He gives 8 away. How many stamps does he have left?

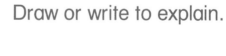

Draw or write to explain.

_____ stamps

9. **Talk About It** Does Henri need to regroup? Why?

 At Home Have your child explain why he or she circled **Yes** in Exercise 2.

Name ______________________________

Writing Math: Create and Solve

Write a subtraction story that has a difference of 5.

____

____

____

____

Draw a picture to go with your story.

Complete the subtraction sentence to solve the problem.

_____ ◯ _____ = 5

Quick Check

Complete the subtraction sentences.

1. 7 tens – 5 tens = _____ tens

   _____ – _____ = _____

2. 9 tens – 6 tens = _____ tens

   _____ – _____ = _____

Use Workmat 5.
Subtract.

3. 45 – 20 = _____   4. 83 – 30 = _____   5. 57 – 10 = _____

Regroup 1 ten.
Write the tens and ones.

6. | 34 | 3 tens 4 ones   Regroup ▷   _____ tens _____ ones

7. | 80 | 8 tens 0 ones   Regroup ▷   _____ tens _____ ones

Decide if you need to regroup.
Circle Yes or No. Write the difference.

	Show the greater number.	Do you need to regroup to subtract?		Subtract the ones. How many tens and ones are left?	What is the difference?
8.	64 – 9	Yes	No	_____ tens _____ ones	
9.	53 – 7	Yes	No	_____ tens _____ ones	
10.	38 – 6	Yes	No	_____ tens _____ ones	

Subtract One-Digit Numbers From Two-Digit Numbers

 MathTracks 2/4
Listen and Understand

Objective
Subtract a one-digit number from a two-digit number with and without regrouping.

Subtract 43 − 5.

Step 1

Show 43. Can you subtract 5 ones?

Workmat 3

Tens	Ones

Tens	Ones
4	3
−	5

Step 2

Regroup 1 ten as 10 ones.

Workmat 3

Tens	Ones

Tens	Ones
3	13
4	3
−	5

Step 3

Subtract the ones. Then, subtract the tens.

Workmat 3

Tens	Ones

Tens	Ones
3	13
4	3
−	5
3	8

Guided Practice

Use Workmat 3 with ▭▭▭▭▭▭▭▭▭▭ and ▯.
Subtract.

1.
Tens	Ones
3	2
−	4

Think
Do I need to regroup to subtract 4 ones from 2 ones?

2.
Tens	Ones
5	0
−	6

3.
Tens	Ones
4	6
−	3

TEST TIPS Explain Your Thinking What does the 10 in the ☐ represent in Exercise 2?

Practice

Remember to regroup when there are not enough ones.

Use Workmat 3 with 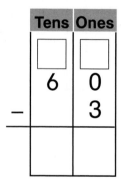 and ▫.
Subtract.

1.

Tens	Ones
4̶ 5	1̶0̶ 0̶
−	4
4	6

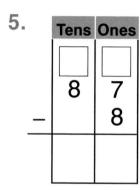
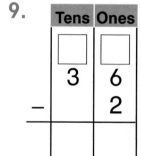

Workmat 3

Tens	Ones

2.

Tens	Ones
6	5
−	8

3.

Tens	Ones
4	3
−	7

4.

Tens	Ones
2	6
−	4

5.

Tens	Ones
8	7
−	8

6.

Tens	Ones
7	9
−	6

7.

Tens	Ones
6	0
−	3

8.

Tens	Ones
7	1
−	5

9.

Tens	Ones
3	6
−	2

10.

Tens	Ones
9	4
−	9

Problem Solving ▶ Mental Math

11. Lin has 85 craft sticks. She gives 20 away. How many sticks does she have left?

Draw or write to explain.

_____ craft sticks

334 three hundred thirty-four

 At Home Tell your child your age. Have your child find the difference between your age and his or her age.

Name_____

Subtract Two-Digit Numbers

 MathTracks 2/5
Listen and Understand

Find 32 − 18.

Objective
Subtract two-digit numbers with and without regrouping.

Step 1
Show 32. Can you subtract 8 ones?

Workmat 3

Tens	Ones

Tens	Ones
3	2
− 1	8

Step 2
Regroup 1 ten as 10 ones.

Workmat 3

Tens	Ones

Tens	Ones
2	12
3	2
− 1	8

Step 3
Subtract the ones.

Workmat 3

Tens	Ones

Tens	Ones
2	12
3	2
− 1	8

Step 4
Subtract the tens.

Workmat 3

Tens	Ones

Tens	Ones
2	12
3	2
− 1	8
	4

Guided Practice

Use Workmat 3 with ▭▭▭▭▭ and ▫.
Subtract.

1.

Tens	Ones
2	5
− 1	6

Think
Do I need to regroup to subtract 6 ones from 5 ones?

2.

Tens	Ones
4	9
− 2	5

3.

Tens	Ones
5	0
− 3	7

TEST TIPS **Explain Your Thinking** How does knowing that 3 tens and 2 ones is the same as 2 tens and 12 ones help you subtract?

Remember to record the number of regrouped tens and ones.

Use Workmat 3 with ▭▭▭▭ and ▫.
Subtract.

1.

Tens	Ones
5	13
6	3
− 2	9
3	4

2.

Tens	Ones
☐	☐
7	5
− 2	8

3.

Tens	Ones
☐	☐
7	3
− 4	2

4.

Tens	Ones
☐	☐
3	5
− 1	3

5.

Tens	Ones
☐	☐
9	0
− 4	7

6.

Tens	Ones
☐	☐
8	9
− 2	7

7.

Tens	Ones
☐	☐
2	4
− 1	9

8.

Tens	Ones
☐	☐
5	8
− 4	2

9.

Tens	Ones
☐	☐
6	2
− 3	6

10.

Tens	Ones
☐	☐
9	3
− 2	9

Problem Solving ▶ Number Sense

11. Show 94 with your blocks. Pick a number to subtract from 94 for which you need to regroup. Complete the number sentence and solve.

Draw or write to explain.

94 − _____ = _____

12. **Talk About It** How did you know you needed to regroup?

At Home Write a two-digit subtraction problem such as 58 − 29. Ask your child to explain how to find the difference.

Name_____

Use a Table

Objective
Use data from a table to solve problems.

Kari collects things she finds around the house.

Item	Number
buttons	43
keys	64
paper clips	29
bottle caps	17

Use the table to solve an addition problem.

How many keys and paper clips does Kari have in all?

Find the information you need in the table.

Think
I need to find a total, so I will add.

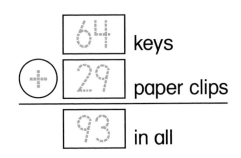

$$
\begin{array}{r}
64 \text{ keys} \\
+\ 29 \text{ paper clips} \\
\hline
93 \text{ in all}
\end{array}
$$

Use the table to solve a subtraction problem.

How many more buttons than bottle caps does Kari have?

Find the information you need in the table.

Think
I need to compare two amounts, so I will subtract.

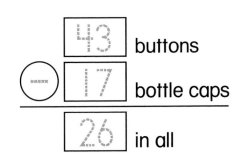

$$
\begin{array}{r}
43 \text{ buttons} \\
-\ 17 \text{ bottle caps} \\
\hline
26 \text{ in all}
\end{array}
$$

The second-grade class brings in items they have collected. The chart shows all the items they have.

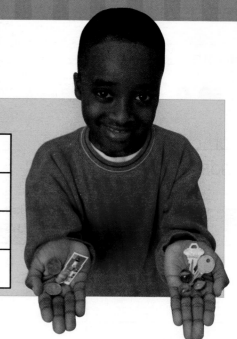

Item	Number
marbles	64
stamps	50
keys	45
pennies	37

Use the table to solve the problem.

1. How many more marbles than stamps does the class have?

   Which numbers should I use?

   Draw or write to explain.

   _____ marbles

2. How many stamps and keys do they collect?

   Do I add or subtract?

   _____ items

Practice

3. 17 of the keys are not silver. The rest of the keys are silver. How many are silver?

   _____ are silver

4. **Multistep** Kaia brings in 18 marbles. Marcus brings in 14 marbles. Cheyenne brings in the rest of the marbles. How many marbles does Cheyenne bring in?

   _____ marbles

Go on

Choose a Strategy

Mr. Blackwell's students bring pictures of bugs to school for a class collection. They put the results in a chart.

Use the data from the table to solve the problem.

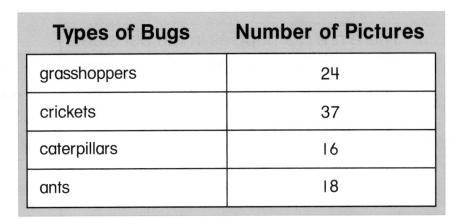

Types of Bugs	Number of Pictures
grasshoppers	24
crickets	37
caterpillars	16
ants	18

Draw or write to explain.

1. Cooper brings 4 more cricket pictures. How many cricket pictures does the class have now?

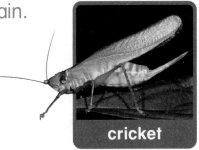

cricket

_____ cricket pictures

2. Simone uses 9 of the grasshopper pictures for a report. How many grasshopper pictures are left?

grasshopper

_____ grasshopper pictures

3. **Multistep** Shakira uses 6 ant pictures for a poster. Levi finds 3 more ant pictures. How many ant pictures does the class have now?

ant

_____ ant pictures

At Home Have your child make a story problem for you using the information in the table.

Listen to your teacher read the problem.
Solve.

1. There are 45 puppies in the pet store. 20 of the puppies are sold. How many puppies are left?

Show your work using pictures, numbers, or words.

_____ puppies

2. Jelani has 19 stickers. Together he and Tommy have 59 stickers. How many stickers does Tommy have?

_____ stickers

Listen to your teacher read the problem.
Choose the correct answer.

3. 28   23   33   15
    ○   ○   ○   ○

4. 27   35   38   43
    ○   ○   ○   ○

Name_____

Subtract.

1.

Tens	Ones
☐	☐
8	4
−	9

2.

Tens	Ones
☐	☐
3	8
−	4

3.

Tens	Ones
☐	☐
6	2
−	8

4.

Tens	Ones
☐	☐
4	9
−	6

5.

Tens	Ones
☐	☐
5	4
− 1	7

6.

Tens	Ones
☐	☐
7	6
− 1	2

7.

Tens	Ones
☐	☐
9	0
− 4	7

8.

Tens	Ones
☐	☐
2	7
− 1	8

9.

Tens	Ones
☐	☐
6	5
−	8

10.

Tens	Ones
☐	☐
3	5
− 1	4

11.

Tens	Ones
☐	☐
4	3
−	6

12.

Tens	Ones
☐	☐
5	7
− 2	8

Use the table to solve the problem.

13. How many more children collect coins than insects?

_____ children

Children's Collections

stamps	38
coins	24
dolls	17
insects	15

Circle the shapes that match the name.

1.

trapezoid

2.

triangle

Write the name of the shape.

3.  _____

4. _____

5. _____

6. 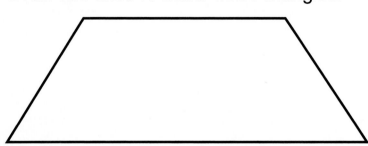 _____

Tricky Triangles

Draw two lines to make three triangles.

Name_____

Vocabulary ⓔ ● Glossary
Complete the sentence.

difference
regroup
subtract

1. I _____ to find out how much is left.

2. You call the answer to a subtraction problem the _____.

3. I can _____ 1 ten as 10 ones to show a number another way.

Concepts and Skills
Complete the subtraction sentence.

4. 8 tens − 4 tens = _____ tens

_____ − _____ = _____

5. 9 tens − 3 tens = _____ tens

_____ − _____ = _____

Subtract.

6. 55
   −20
   ____

7. 99
   −50
   ____

8. 72
   −40
   ____

9. 58
   −10
   ____

10. 46
    −30
    ____

Use Workmat 3 with ▭▭▭▭▭ and ▫ .
Regroup 1 ten. Write the tens and ones.

11. 68 _____ tens _____ ones Regroup ⟩ _____ tens _____ ones

12. 45 _____ tens _____ ones Regroup ⟩ _____ tens _____ ones

13. 60 _____ tens _____ ones Regroup ⟩ _____ tens _____ ones

Decide if you need to regroup.
Circle **Yes** or **No**.
Write the difference.

14. $56 - 8$

Yes   No   _____

15. $67 - 5$

Yes   No   _____

Subtract.

16.
$$\begin{array}{r} 85 \\ -\ 9 \\ \hline \end{array}$$

17.
$$\begin{array}{r} 56 \\ -35 \\ \hline \end{array}$$

18.
$$\begin{array}{r} 43 \\ -15 \\ \hline \end{array}$$

19.
$$\begin{array}{r} 30 \\ -\ 8 \\ \hline \end{array}$$

20.
$$\begin{array}{r} 18 \\ -10 \\ \hline \end{array}$$

21.
$$\begin{array}{r} 47 \\ -24 \\ \hline \end{array}$$

22.
$$\begin{array}{r} 60 \\ -36 \\ \hline \end{array}$$

23.
$$\begin{array}{r} 25 \\ -13 \\ \hline \end{array}$$

Problem Solving
Use the table to solve.

Item	Number Collected
marbles	53
pipe cleaners	18
rocks	26
keys	34

24. How many more marbles than rocks did the class collect?

Draw or write to explain.

_____ more marbles

25. How many keys and pipe cleaners did they collect?

_____ keys and pipe cleaners

Using Two-Digit Subtraction

CHAPTER 13

INVESTIGATION

Use the picture to tell a two-digit subtraction story.

Flying Colors

Find the difference.
Color by number.

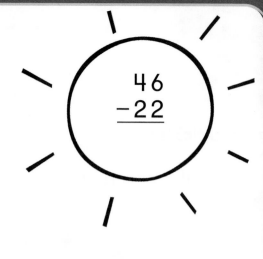

$$\begin{array}{r} 46 \\ -22 \\ \hline \end{array}$$

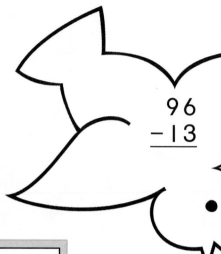

$$\begin{array}{r} 96 \\ -13 \\ \hline \end{array}$$

$$\begin{array}{r} 35 \\ -20 \\ \hline \end{array}$$

41	red
15	blue
60	green
24	yellow
35	brown
52	purple
71	light green
83	orange

$$\begin{array}{r} 83 \\ -42 \\ \hline \end{array}$$

$$\begin{array}{r} 71 \\ -36 \\ \hline \end{array}$$

$$\begin{array}{r} 87 \\ -16 \\ \hline \end{array}$$

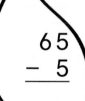

$$\begin{array}{r} 65 \\ -\ 5 \\ \hline \end{array}$$

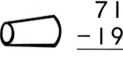

$$\begin{array}{r} 71 \\ -19 \\ \hline \end{array}$$

$$\begin{array}{r} 61 \\ -\ 9 \\ \hline \end{array}$$

$$\begin{array}{r} 85 \\ -14 \\ \hline \end{array}$$

$$\begin{array}{r} 85 \\ -50 \\ \hline \end{array}$$

Rewrite to Subtract

MathTracks 2/6
Listen and Understand

Objective
Rewrite subtraction problems in vertical form.

Find 85 − 59.

Step 1

Rewrite 85 − 59. Line up the ones and the tens.

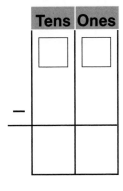

Tens	Ones
8	5
− 5	9

Step 2

Subtract the ones. Subtract the tens.

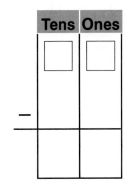

Tens	Ones
7	15
8	5
− 5	9
2	6

Remember to regroup.

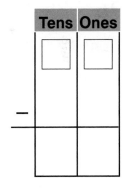

Guided Practice

Write the numbers in vertical form. Subtract.

1. 46 − 7

Tens	Ones
−	

Think
Do I write the 7 in the ones or the tens column?

2. 63 − 7

Tens	Ones
−	

3. 84 − 55

Tens	Ones
−	

4. 81 − 32

Tens	Ones
−	

5. 77 − 58

Tens	Ones
−	

6. 78 − 69

Tens	Ones
−	

7. 65 − 4

Tens	Ones
−	

TEST TIPS **Explain Your Thinking** Brenda rewrites 72 − 6. She subtracts and gets a difference of 12. What did she do wrong?

Remember
Line up the ones
and the tens.

Write the numbers in vertical form. Subtract.

1. 36 – 19

Tens	Ones
2	16
3	6
– 1	9
1	7

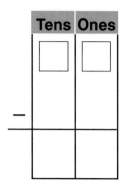

2. 58 – 24

Tens	Ones
□	□
–	

3. 68 – 32

Tens	Ones
□	□
–	

4. 64 – 47

Tens	Ones
□	□
–	

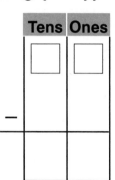

5. 42 – 3

Tens	Ones
□	□
–	

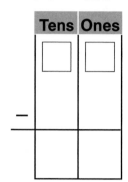

6. 71 – 25

Tens	Ones
□	□
–	

7. 38 – 17

Tens	Ones
□	□
–	

8. 96 – 34

Tens	Ones
□	□
–	

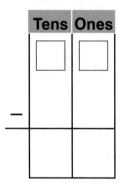

9. 81 – 4

Tens	Ones
□	□
–	

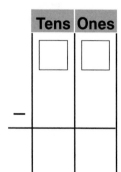

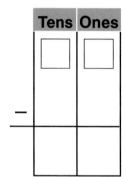

10. 60 – 35

Tens	Ones
□	□
–	

11. 45 – 27

Tens	Ones
□	□
–	

Problem Solving ▶ Reasoning

Draw or write to explain.

12. Tanya has 45 paper clips.
She uses 17 to make a necklace.
How many paper clips does she
have left?

_____ paper clips

At Home Have your child show you how to rewrite
53 – 16 and 63 – 7 and then find the differences.

Name_____

More Two-Digit Subtraction

Objective
Practice two-digit subtraction with and without regrouping.

Pete sees 42 birds at his birdhouse.
16 of the birds are blue.
How many birds are not blue?

Subtract to solve the problem.

Step 1

Line up the ones and tens.

Tens	Ones
☐	☐
4	2
− 1	6

Step 2

Regroup 1 ten as 10 ones. Subtract the ones.

Tens	Ones
3	12
4̸	2̸
− 1	6
	6

Step 3

Subtract the tens.

Tens	Ones
3	12
4̸	2̸
− 1	6
2	6

26 birds are not blue.

Guided Practice

Subtract.

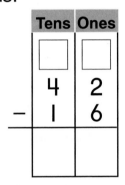

Think
I cannot subtract 5 ones from 0 ones. I need to regroup.

1.
☐	☐
5	0
− 3	5

2.
☐	☐
4	1
− 1	6

3.
☐	☐
7	4
− 2	5

4.
☐	☐
5	5
−	7

Write the numbers in vertical form. Subtract.

5. 65 − 8

Tens	Ones
☐	☐
−	

6. 32 − 11

Tens	Ones
☐	☐
−	

7. 87 − 18

Tens	Ones
☐	☐
−	

8. 75 − 9

Tens	Ones
☐	☐
−	

TEST TIPS **Explain Your Thinking** Do you ever have to regroup to make 19 ones when you subtract? Why?

When you subtract, ask yourself if you need to regroup tens as ones.

Subtract.

1. ☐☐
       9 | 4
    − 6 | 2
       3 | 2

2. ☐☐
       3 | 1
    − 2 | 6

3. ☐☐
       3 | 4
    − 1 | 5

4. ☐☐
       4 | 7
    − 1 | 6

5. ☐☐
       9 | 9
    − 9 | 7

6.   59
    − 7

7.   73
    − 56

8.   87
    − 18

9.   63
    − 27

10.   75
    − 36

Write the numbers in vertical form. Subtract.

11. 52 − 18

Tens	Ones
☐	☐

12. 40 − 9

Tens	Ones
☐	☐

13. 96 − 49

Tens	Ones
☐	☐

14. 81 − 37

Tens	Ones
☐	☐

Algebra Readiness ▶ Missing Addends

15. Someone spills juice on the craft fair's records. Find the numbers you cannot read.

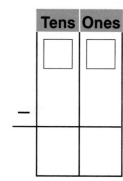

Type of Craft	Number Sold Each Day		
	Saturday	Sunday	Total
Birdhouse	73	21	
Potholder	67		94
Picture Frame	71	11	

_____ birdhouses

_____ potholders sold Sunday

_____ total picture frames

At Home Ask your child to find these differences: 52 − 37 and 67 − 19. Then ask him or her which difference is greater.

Name_____

Estimate Differences

 MathTracks 2/7
Listen and Understand

When you do not need an exact answer,
you can **estimate.**

Estimate the difference. 35 − 22.

Step 1

Round each number to the nearest ten.

22 is closer to 20.
Round down.

35 is in the middle between
30 and 40. Round up.

20 21 22 23 24 25 26 27 28 29 30 31 32 33 34 35 36 37 38 39 40

Step 2

Subtract the tens to estimate the difference.

$40 - 20 = 20$

Guided Practice

Round each number to the nearest ten.
Estimate the difference.

30 31 32 33 34 35 36 37 38 39 40 41 42 43 44 45 46 47 48 49 50

Think
Both numbers have 5 or
more ones, so I round up.

1. 49 − 35

_____ − _____ = _____

2. 41 − 32

_____ − _____ = _____

3. 45 − 28

_____ − _____ = _____

TEST TIPS **Explain Your Thinking** How did you find the nearest ten for
each number in Exercise 3?

Remember to round down if the number has less than five ones.

Round each number to the nearest ten.
Estimate the difference.

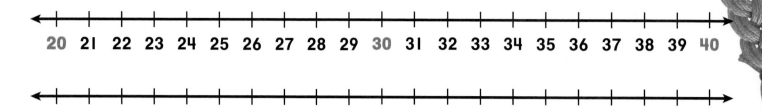

20 21 22 23 24 25 26 27 28 29 30 31 32 33 34 35 36 37 38 39 40

40 41 42 43 44 45 46 47 48 49 50 51 52 53 54 55 56 57 58 59 60

1. 58 − 42

___60___ − ___40___ = ___20___

2. 53 − 41

___ − ___ = ___

3. 49 − 43

___ − ___ = ___

4. 57 − 34

___ − ___ = ___

5. 59 − 47

___ − ___ = ___

6. 44 − 41

___ − ___ = ___

7. 45 − 18

___ − ___ = ___

8. 37 − 21

___ − ___ = ___

9. 49 − 33

___ − ___ = ___

10. 46 − 24

___ − ___ = ___

11. 57 − 21

___ − ___ = ___

12. 72 − 24

___ − ___ = ___

Problem Solving ▶ Reasoning

Draw or write to explain.

13. Karen estimates 52 − 13 this way.

50 − 10 = 40

Karen subtracts 52 − 13 this way.

52 − 13 = 5

Is her exact answer reasonable?
Explain why.

At Home Ask your child to demonstrate how to round
to the nearest ten and estimate to find a difference.

Subtract From 99

2 Players

What You Need: Bag with Number Cards 0–25, paper, and pencil

How to Play

1. Write the number 99 at the top of your paper.

2. Take turns drawing a number card from the bag.

3. Subtract your number from 99.

4. Take turns drawing new numbers from the bag. Subtract each new number from the last difference on your paper.

5. The player with the lesser difference after four turns wins.

Quick Check

Write the numbers in vertical form. Subtract.

1. 55 – 17

Tens	Ones
–	

2. 81 – 4

Tens	Ones
–	

3. 49 – 25

Tens	Ones
–	

4. 67 – 36

Tens	Ones
–	

Subtract.

5. 76
  −24

6. 46
  −37

7. 85
  −56

8. 60
  −24

9. 92
  −37

Round each number to the nearest ten.
Estimate the difference.

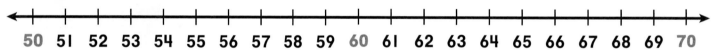

50 51 52 53 54 55 56 57 58 59 60 61 62 63 64 65 66 67 68 69 70

10. 67 – 52

_____ – _____ = _____

11. 68 – 55

_____ – _____ = _____

Social Studies Connection

Postage Stamps

The first stamps were used in the United States over 150 years ago. In 1918, it cost 3¢ to mail a letter. How much more does it cost to mail a letter today than in 1918?

_____

WEEKLY WR **READER** eduplace.com/kids/mw/

Name_____

Choose a Way to Subtract

Different ways to subtract:
- mental math
- calculator
- tens and ones blocks
- paper and pencil

Choose a way to find $55 - 39$.

I can use a calculator or pencil and paper to solve this.

Guided Practice

Circle the way that you would use to subtract.
Find the difference.

1. $36 - 10 =$ _____

   mental math

   calculator

   Think
   Can I count back in my head to subtract 10 from 36?

2. $41 - 32 =$ _____

   tens and ones blocks

   mental math

3. $87 - 43 =$ _____
   paper and pencil

   calculator

4. $58 - 30 =$ _____
   mental math

   calculator

5. $96 - 37 =$ _____
   mental math

   calculator

Explain how you find the difference.

6. $47 - 13$ _____

_____

TEST TIPS **Explain Your Thinking** Why is it faster to use mental math than a calculator to find $73 - 30$?

Remember to choose the way that works best for you.

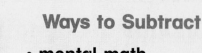

Ways to Subtract

- mental math
- calculator
- tens and ones
- paper and pencil

Choose a way to subtract.
Explain how you find the difference.

1. 42 – 19

_____

_____

_____

2. 58 – 7

_____

_____

_____

3. 84 – 37

_____

_____

_____

4. 75 – 43

_____

_____

_____

Problem Solving ▶ Mental Math

Draw or write to explain.

5. Billy has 80 buttons. He gives 30 away. Sonya asks Billy for 60 buttons. Does he have enough to give her? Explain how you know.

At Home Have your child show different ways to subtract 58 – 20 and explain which way he or she would use.

Use Addition to Check Subtraction

MathTracks 2/8
Listen and Understand

You can add to check your subtraction.

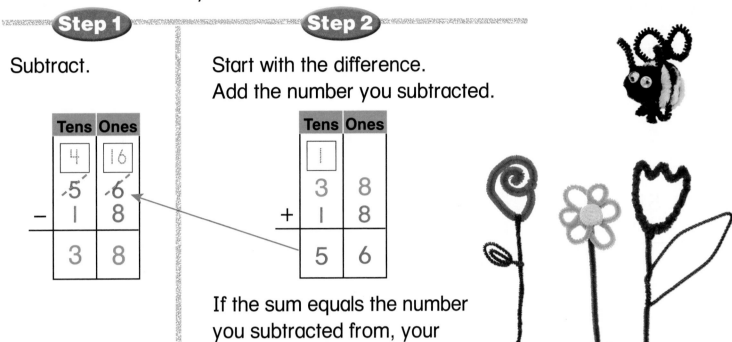

Step 1

Subtract.

Tens	Ones
4 16	
5	6
− 1	8
3	8

Step 2

Start with the difference.
Add the number you subtracted.

Tens	Ones
1	
3	8
+ 1	8
5	6

If the sum equals the number you subtracted from, your answer is correct.

Guided Practice

Subtract. Check by adding.

1. 32
   −19

   + ☐
   ☐
   ───
   ☐

Think
13 is the difference.
I add 13 and 19 to check.

2. 81
   −66

   ☐
   + ☐
   ───
   ☐

3. 72
   −64

   ☐
   + ☐
   ───
   ☐

TEST TIPS **Explain Your Thinking** Why can you use addition to check subtraction?

Add the difference and the number you subtracted to check.

Subtract.
Check by adding.

1. 68
   −42
   ‾‾‾
    26

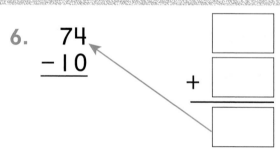

```
   26
+  42
‾‾‾‾‾
   68
```

2. 40
   − 5

```
+
```

3. 54
   −19

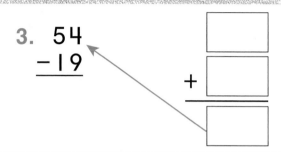

```
+
```

4. 85
   − 6

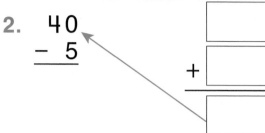

```
+
```

5. 49
   −28

```
+
```

6. 74
   −10

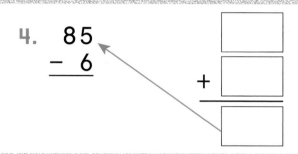

```
+
```

7. 53
   − 7

```
+
```

8. 98
   −51

```
+
```

Algebra Readiness ▶ Variables

9. $43 + \triangle = 46$

What is $\triangle$? _____

10. $46 - \blacksquare = 3$

What is $\blacksquare$? _____

At Home Ask your child to show you how to use addition to check a subtraction problem such as 58 − 29.

Name_____

Choose the Operation

MathTracks 2/9
Listen and Understand

Objective
Decide when to use addition or subtraction to solve a problem.

Use addition to find how many in all.

There are 25 blue bird houses for sale.
There are 17 red bird houses for sale.
How many bird houses are for sale?

Whole
42

Part	Part
25	17

Think
I add the parts to find the whole.

___42___ bird houses

Use subtraction to find one part.

Only 13 blue bird houses get sold.
How many blue bird houses do not get sold?

Whole
25

Part	Part
13	12

Think
I know the whole and one of the parts. I can subtract to find the other part.

___12___ blue bird houses

You use subtraction to compare two amounts.

How many more blue bird houses are there than red bird houses?

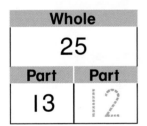

___25___ – ___17___ = ___8___ bird houses

Think
I need to compare the number of red and blue bird houses so I will subtract.

Find the parts and whole to solve.
Write the answer.

1. There are 47 children in the class.
   19 children make crafts.
   How many children do not
   make crafts?

   Think
   I know the total
   and one part.
   I need to find the
   other part.

Whole	
Part	Part

   _28_ children

2. There are 32 potholders and
   17 oven mitts for sale. How
   many potholders and
   oven mitts are for sale?

   Think
   I need to find how
   many in all.

Whole	
Part	Part

   _____ potholders
   and oven mitts

Practice

3. There are 23 picture frames for sale.
   8 are sold. How many picture frames
   are left?

Whole	
Part	Part

   _____ picture frames

4. The students invite 26 people on
   Monday and 19 people on Tuesday.
   How many people are invited on
   both days?

Whole	
Part	Part

   _____ people

Go on

Name_____

Choose a Strategy

Strategies

Draw a Picture
Use Models to Act It Out
Write a Number Sentence

Solve.

1. There are 17 students in Ms. Ramirez's class. 8 sell pencil holders. How many students do not sell pencil holders?

Draw or write to explain.

pencil holder

_____ students

---

2. Max makes 35 bracelets. Emily makes 18 bracelets. How many more bracelets did Max make than Emily?

_____ bracelets

bracelet

---

3. 47 girls made puppets. 18 boys made puppets. How many more girls than boys made puppets?

_____ girls

puppets

---

4. **Multistep** Casey makes 4 pinwheels. His friend gives him 1 more. Each pinwheel has two circles. How many circles in all?

pinwheel

_____ circles

At Home Tell your child a story problem that ends with the question, "Who has more?" Then ask him or her whether they should add or subtract to solve.

three hundred sixty-one **361**

 Problem-Solving for Tests

Listening Skills

 TEST PREP

Listen to your teacher read the problem. Solve.

1. There are 32 chipmunks and 8 deer in a field. 15 of the animals leave. How many animals are left in the field?

Show your work using pictures, numbers, or words.

_____ animals

2. Mickey has 2 quarters and 3 pennies. He gives 28¢ to his little sister. How much money does Mickey have left?

_____ ¢

Listen to your teacher read the problem. Choose the correct answer.

3. about 20 ○   about 30 ○   about 40 ○   about 50 ○

4. 30 minutes ○   1 hour ○   2 hours ○   3 hours ○

Name ______________________________

Quick Check

Ways to Subtract
- **mental math**
- **calculator**
- **tens and ones**
- **paper and pencil**

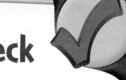

Choose a way to subtract.
Explain how you find the difference.

1. 57 − 24

____
____
____

2. 69 − 7

____
____
____

Subtract.
Check by adding.

3.
$$\begin{array}{r} 92 \\ -27 \\ \hline \end{array}$$

$$\begin{array}{r} \square \\ +\ \square \\ \hline \square \end{array}$$

4.
$$\begin{array}{r} 65 \\ -\ 8 \\ \hline \end{array}$$

$$\begin{array}{r} \square \\ +\ \square \\ \hline \square \end{array}$$

Add or subtract to solve.
Write the number sentence.

5. Claudia makes 32 potholders for the crafts show. She sells 15 potholders. How many potholders does she have left?

_____ ◯ _____ = _____ potholders

Write the name of the solid shape. Circle the objects that match the solid shape.

cube	sphere	rectangular prism
cylinder	cone	square pyramid

1.

_____

2.

_____

3.

_____

Write the names of the two solid shapes in the picture.

4.

_____   _____

Science Connection

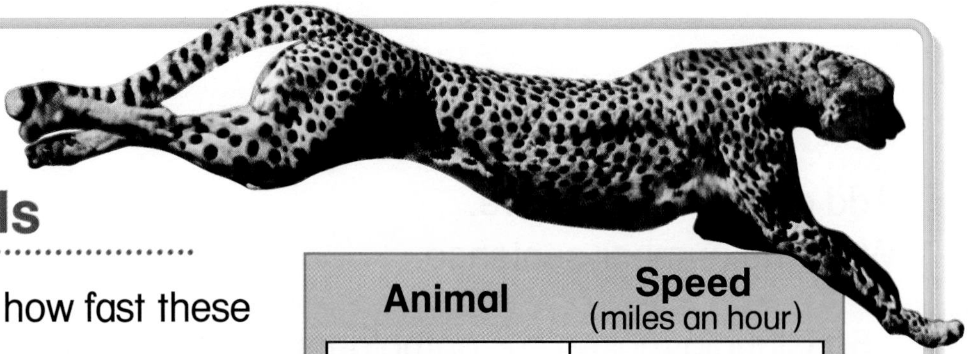

Speedy Animals

The chart shows about how fast these animals can run.

How much faster can an antelope run than a hyena?

_____ miles an hour

Animal	Speed (miles an hour)
Cheetah	70
Antelope	60
Hyena	40
Grizzly Bear	30

WEEKLY (WR) READER eduplace.com/kids/mw/

Chapter Review/Test

Vocabulary _e • Glossary_

Complete the sentence.

| estimate |
| round |
| difference |

1. When I do not need an exact answer I can _____.

2. The _____ is the answer to a subtraction problem.

3. I _____ numbers to help me estimate.

Concepts and Skills

Rewrite the numbers. Subtract.

4. 56 – 8

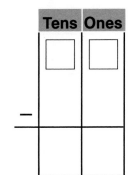

5. 32 – 11

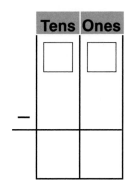

6. 78 – 29

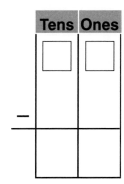

7. 40 – 22

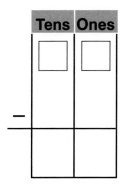

Round each number to the nearest ten.

Estimate the difference.

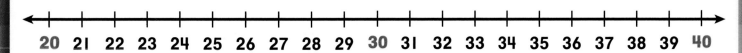

20 21 22 23 24 25 26 27 28 29 30 31 32 33 34 35 36 37 38 39 40

8. 39 – 21

___ – ___ = ___

9. 32 – 14

___ – ___ = ___

10. 25 – 12

___ – ___ = ___

11. 37 – 25

___ – ___ = ___

Subtract.

12. 67
    −34

13. 23
    −15

14. 92
    −71

15. 50
    −28

Choose a way to subtract.
Explain how you find the difference.

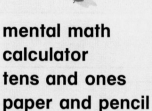

mental math
calculator
tens and ones
paper and pencil

16. 76 − 30

_____

_____

_____

17. 54 − 29

_____

_____

_____

Subtract.
Check by adding.

18. 80
    −43

   □
 + □
 ___
   □

19. 45
    −26

   □
 + □
 ___
   □

Problem Solving

Add or subtract to solve.
Complete the boxes.

20. There are 56 children at the craft
    sale. 29 of the children are boys.
    The rest of the children are girls.
    How many girls are at the craft sale?

Whole	
Part	Part

_____ girls

Name_____

Sorting Shells

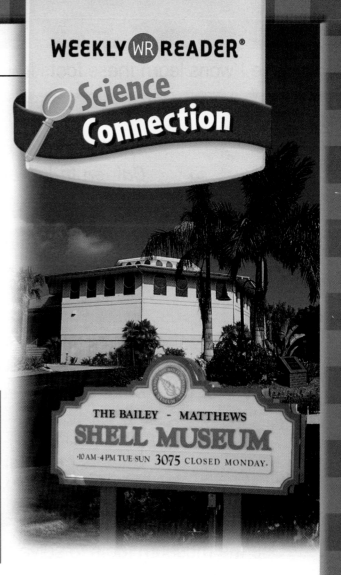

The Kwan family visits The Bailey-Matthews Shell Museum in Sanibel, Florida. This is the largest shell museum in the United States.

The Kwans take a museum tour. Then they sort and count shells on the beach.

Use the table to answer the questions.

Type of Shell	Number of Shells Counted
Whelk	42
Clam	18
Snail	23
Cockle	6

1. How many whelk and clam shells do they count altogether?

Draw or write to explain.

_____ shells

2. How many more clam shells than cockle shells do they count?

_____ clam shells

3. Multistep How many more whelk shells than clam and snail shells do they count?

_____ whelk shell

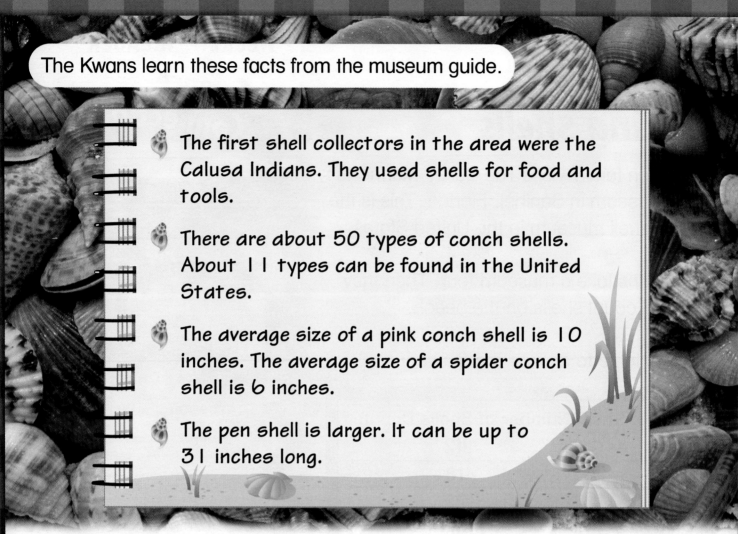

The Kwans learn these facts from the museum guide.

The first shell collectors in the area were the Calusa Indians. They used shells for food and tools.

There are about 50 types of conch shells. About 11 types can be found in the United States.

The average size of a pink conch shell is 10 inches. The average size of a spider conch shell is 6 inches.

The pen shell is larger. It can be up to 31 inches long.

Use the museum facts to solve.

1. About how many types of conch shells are not found in the United States?

Draw or write to explain.

about _____ types

2. About how much larger is the pink conch shell than the spider conch shell?

about _____ inches

3. About how much larger can a pen shell be than an average spider conch shell?

about _____ inches

 Technology
Visit *Education Place* at
eduplace.com/kids/mw/
to learn more about this topic.

368 three hundred sixty-eight

Name_____

Vocabulary (*e* • Glossary)

Complete the sentence.

	subtract
	difference
	regroup

1. You can _____ 1 ten as 10 ones to show a number another way.

2. When you _____, you take one number away from another to find a difference.

3. The _____ is the answer to a subtraction problem.

Concepts and Skills

Complete the subtraction sentences.

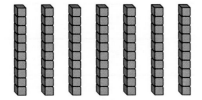   

4. 7 tens − 5 tens = _____ tens

_____ − _____ = _____

5. 6 tens − 3 tens = _____ tens

_____ − _____ = _____

Decide if you need to regroup.
Circle **Yes** or **No**.
Write the difference.

6. 48 − 6

Yes   No   _____

7. 32 − 4

Yes   No   _____

Subtract.

8. 61
  − 20

9. 53
  − 14

10. 75
   − 28

Subtract.
Check by adding.

11.   60
     − 25

□
+ □
───
□

12.   34
     − 16

□
+ □
───
□

Problem Solving

Use the table to solve.

Marble Color	Number in the Box
red	12
yellow	47
green	53
purple	29

13. How many more green marbles than yellow marbles are in the box?

Draw or write to explain.

_____ more green marbles

14. How many more purple marbles than red marbles are in the box?

_____ more purple marbles

Add or subtract to solve.
Complete the boxes.

15. There are 72 birds. 38 of the birds are robins. The rest of the birds are bluebirds. How many bluebirds are there?

Whole

Part	Part

_____ bluebirds

Performance Assessment

1. 72 − 37.

> Show your work with pictures, numbers, or words.
>
> _____

2. Use the number line. Round each number to the nearest ten. Estimate the difference.

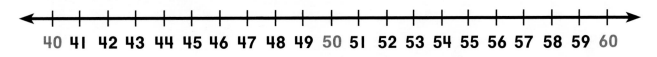

40 41 42 43 44 45 46 47 48 49 50 51 52 53 54 55 56 57 58 59 60

$$\begin{array}{r} 58 \\ -\ 43 \\ \hline \end{array}$$

> Show your work with pictures, numbers, or words.
>
> _____

3. The toy museum has **34** teddy bears and **28** dolls. How many more teddy bears than dolls does the museum have?

Show your work with pictures, numbers, or words.

_____ more teddy bears

Guess and Check to Add Money

Each child has 80¢ to spend at the toy shop.
Guess and then check to find what the
child buys.

sticker 8¢

26¢ airplane

55¢ necklace

31¢ fire engine

yo-yo 15¢

1. Timo has 72¢ left. What did
   he buy?

Draw or write to explain.

_____

2. Kyle has 23¢ left. Which 2 items
   did he buy?

_____

_____

3. Pancho has 10¢ left. Which 2
   items did he buy?

_____

_____

4. **Write Your Own** Write a problem about the toy shop
   on another piece of paper. Ask a friend to solve it.

Technology
Visit *Education Place* at
eduplace.com/kids/mw/
for brain teasers.

Calculator Sum and Difference Race

What You Need: 8 yellow counters for Player 1, 8 red counters for Player 2, calculator

How to Play

1. Player 1 starts at the top of the game board. Player 2 starts at the side.

2. Choose 2 numbers from the list. Then use a calculator to find the sum or difference. If it matches an answer on the game board, put a counter on it. Only 1 counter can be on any one space.

3. Take turns until one player creates a path from one side to the other.

List

6	11
7	
25	14
33	
47	58
66	75

Player 1			
20	13	41	89
91	89	36	68
72	80	19	8
31	59	47	22

Player 2 (left side) / Player 2 (right side)

Player 1 (bottom)

Test-Taking Tips
. . . .

Read each answer choice carefully
before you answer the question.

Check to be sure you marked the
correct answer choice.

Multiple Choice

Fill in the ○ for the correct answer.

1. Mark another way to show 45.

   ○   3 tens 6 ones

   ○   5 tens 4 ones

   ○   3 tens 15 ones

   ○   4 tens 15 ones

3. 49 − 20 = ☐

   | 19 | 20 | 29 | 30 |
   | ○ | ○ | ○ | ○ |

2. Keisha has 25 soccer medals.
   Enrico has 19 basketball medals.
   How many medals do they have in
   all?

   | 26 | 44 | 45 | 54 |
   | ○ | ○ | ○ | ○ |

4. Mark the number that comes
   between.

   25 ☐ 42

   | 24 | 36 | 46 | 52 |
   | ○ | ○ | ○ | ○ |

Fill in the ○ for the correct answer.
NH means Not Here.

Solve.

5. Find the sum.

$$\begin{array}{r} 64 \\ + 26 \\ \hline \end{array}$$

32	82	90	NH
○	○	○	○

8. Subtract to find the missing addend. Write the subtraction sentence.

43 + ☐ = 48

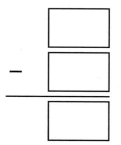

6. Estimate the difference.

53 − 29

about 20	about 40	about 70	about 80
○	○	○	○

9. Complete the fact family.

9 + 7 = _____

____ + ____ = _____

____ − ____ = _____

____ − ____ = _____

7. Find the difference.

$$\begin{array}{r} 92 \\ - 75 \\ \hline \end{array}$$

17	23	27	NH
○	○	○	○

10. Solve. Write an addition sentence to check your answer.

$$\begin{array}{r} 44 \\ - 18 \\ \hline \end{array}$$

____ + ____ = _____

Test Prep on the Net
Visit *Education Place* at
eduplace.com/kids/mw/
for more test prep practice.

Money and Time

From the Read-Aloud Anthology

General Store

by Rachel Field

illustrated by Holly Berry

Access Prior Knowledge

This poem will help you review
- Pennies, nickels, and dimes
- Showing amounts of money

Some day I'm going to have a store
With a tinkly bell hung over the door,
With real glass cases and counters wide
And drawers all spilly with things inside.

I'll fix the window and dust each shelf,
And take the money in all myself,
It will be my store and I will say:
"What can I do for you to-day?"

Name_____

These items are sold in the General Store.
Draw coins to show the amount.

1.

30¢

2.

26¢

3.

9¢

Use the story and pictures on pages 377b and 377c.
Write the price on the tag.
Draw coins to show the amount.

4.

¢

5.

¢

How much do you need to buy both? _____ ¢

MATH at Home

Dear Family,

My class is starting Unit 6. I will be learning about money and time. These two pages show some of what I will learn and have activities for us to do together.

From. _____

Vocabulary

These are some words I will use in this unit.

cent sign	The sign used to show cents (¢)
dollar sign	The symbol used to show dollars ($)
decimal point	The dot used to separate dollars and cents
second	A unit of time; there are 60 seconds in one minute.

minute	A unit of time equal to 60 seconds
hour	A unit of time equal to 60 minutes
half-hour	A unit of time equal to 30 minutes
quarter-hour	A unit of time equal to 15 minutes

Some other words I will use are **calendar**, **dime**, **equal amount**, **nickel**, **penny**, **quarter**, **half-dollar**, and **dollar**.

Vocabulary Activity

Let's work together to complete these sentences.

1. A _____ is used to show cents.

2. A _____ is equal to 15 minutes.

3. A _____ is a dot used to separate dollars and cents.

Turn the page for more.

How To tell time to five minutes

In this unit, I will be learning how to tell time to the hour, half-hour, quarter-hour, and five minutes. This is an example of how I will be learning to tell time to five minutes.

Sometimes, you can skip count by 5s to tell time.

15 minutes after 1

hour → 1 : 15 ← minutes
_____ after the
hour

40 minutes after 3

3 : 40

Literature

These books link to the math in this unit. We can look for them at the library.

I Live in Tokyo
written and illustrated
by Mari Takabayashi
(Houghton Mifflin, 2001)

**Alexander, Who Used to
Be Rich Last Sunday**
Judith Viorst

Bunny Money
Rosemary Wells

Let's read together!

Technology

We can visit *Education Place* at **eduplace.com/parents/mw/** for the Math Lingo game, the *e* • Glossary, and more games and activities to do together.

Counting Money

INVESTIGATION

What can you buy with 12¢?

50¢

2¢

12¢

12¢

3¢

10¢

5¢

20¢

10¢

7¢

25¢

Cat Coins

Listen to each story.

Use and  to act out each story.

Name _____

Pennies, Nickels, and Dimes

Find the value of the coins by skip counting and counting on.

Start with the coin of the greatest value.

Remember that **¢** is a **cent sign.**

Objective
Skip count and count on to find the value of a set of coins.

Vocabulary
dime   nickel   penny
cent sign (¢)

dime 10¢   **nickel** 5¢   **penny** 1¢

Count on by 10.   Count on by 5.   Count on by 1.

__10__ ¢   __20__ ¢   __25__ ¢   __30__ ¢   __31__ ¢   __32__ ¢

The value is __32__ ¢.

Think
I can skip count by
10s to start.

Guided Practice

Count on to find the value of the coins.

1.

_____ ¢   _____ ¢   _____ ¢   _____ ¢   _____ ¢

_____ ¢
total

2.
    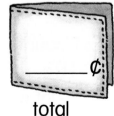

_____ ¢   _____ ¢   _____ ¢   _____ ¢

_____ ¢
total

TEST TIPS **Explain Your Thinking** How does knowing that one dime is 10¢ help you count?

Remember to count on by 10s, 5s, and 1s.

Count on to find the value of the coins.

1.

____10____ ¢   ____20____ ¢   ____30____ ¢   ____35____ ¢

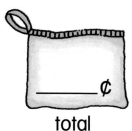

35 ¢
total

2.

_____ ¢ _____ ¢ _____ ¢ _____ ¢ _____ ¢

_____ ¢
total

3.

_____ ¢   _____ ¢   _____ ¢   _____ ¢

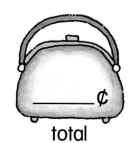

_____ ¢
total

4.

_____ ¢ _____ ¢ _____ ¢ _____ ¢ _____ ¢ _____ ¢

_____ ¢
total

Problem Solving ▶ Reasoning

5. I count my coins like this:
10¢, 15¢, 20¢, 21¢, 22¢.
What coins do I have?

Draw or write to explain.

_____ dime   _____ nickels

_____ pennies

At Home Ask your child to skip count and count on to find the value of dimes, nickels, and pennies totaling less than $1.00.

Name_____

Quarters and Half-Dollars

A set of coins may have a **half-dollar** and a **quarter.**

Objective
Identify a quarter and half-dollar; count on to find the value of a group of coins.

Vocabulary
half-dollar
quarter

half-dollar 50¢   quarter 25¢

Find the value of the coins.
Start with the coin of the greatest value.

____50____¢   ____75____¢   ____85____¢   The value is ____85____¢.

Guided Practice

Count on to find the value of the coins.

1.          **Think**
I need to count
on by 25s.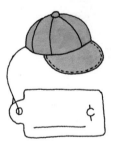

_____¢   _____¢   _____¢   total

2.

_____¢   _____¢   _____¢   _____¢   total

TEST TIPS **Explain Your Thinking** Why do you start counting with 50¢
in Exercise 2?

Count on to find the value of the coins.

Start counting with 50¢ when there is a half-dollar.

1.

_50_ ¢ _75_ ¢

75 ¢

total

2.

_____¢ _____¢ _____¢ _____¢ _____¢

¢

total

3.

_____¢ _____¢ _____¢ _____¢

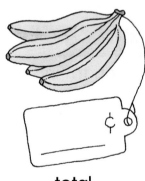

¢

total

Problem Solving ▶ Number Sense

4. Raoul can count all of his coins by tens. He has 60¢. What coins does he have?

Draw or write to explain.

_____

 At Home Ask your child how he or she would count on to find the total value of 3 quarters, two dimes, and a penny.

Name_____

Count Coins

MathTracks 2 / 10
Listen and Understand

  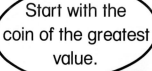 

Objective
Count on to find the value of a set of coins.

Find the value of the coins.

Step 1

First, put the coins in order to find the value.

Start with the coin of the greatest value.

Step 2

Then, count on to find the value.

___25___¢   ___50___¢   ___75___¢   ___85___¢   ___90___¢

The total value is ___90___¢.

Guided Practice

Use coins.
Count on to find the value of the coins.

1.

Think
I start at 50¢ and count on.

_____¢

2.

_____¢

TEST TIPS **Explain Your Thinking** Why does it help to have coins in order from the greatest to the least value when you count?

Remember to start with the coin of the greatest value.

Use coins.
Count on to find the value of the coins.

1.

_53_ ¢

2.

_____ ¢

3.

_____ ¢

4.

_____ ¢

5.

_____ ¢

6.

_____ ¢

Go on

Name_____

Use coins.

Count on to find the value of the coins.

7.

_____¢

8.

_____¢

9.

_____¢

10.

_____¢

Problem Solving ▶ Visual Thinking

11. Rachel has 3 quarters. Brian has 7 dimes.
Draw each child's coins. Circle the group
of coins with the greater value.

Rachel	Brian

At Home Find items advertised for 99¢ or less. Ask your
child to tell which coins could be used to buy each item.

Quick Check

Count on to find the value of the coins.

1.

_____ ¢ _____ ¢ _____ ¢ _____ ¢ _____ ¢ _____ ¢

2.

_____ ¢ _____ ¢ _____ ¢ _____ ¢

Use coins. Count on to find the value of the coins.

3.

_____ ¢

4.

_____ ¢

Social Studies
Connection

State Quarters

In 1999, the U.S. Mint started making state quarters. By 2008, there will be a quarter for each of the 50 states. Does your state have a quarter yet? Which state quarters have you seen?

WEEKLY WR **READER** eduplace.com/kids/mw/

One Dollar

MathTracks 2/11
Listen and Understand

100¢ has the same value as one **dollar.**

Use a **dollar sign** and a **decimal point**

when you write one dollar.

Objective
Identify coin combinations greater than and equal to one dollar.

Vocabulary
dollar
dollar sign
decimal point

one dollar   one dollar

100¢ or $1.00   100¢ or $1.00

↑   ↑
dollar sign   decimal point

Guided Practice

Draw more coins to make one dollar.
Write the amount.

Think
2 quarters equal 50¢. How many more quarters do I need?

Use quarters.

1.

_100_ ¢

$_1.00_

Use dimes.

2.

_____ ¢

$__.___

TEST TIPS **Explain Your Thinking** What other coins could you use to show one dollar?

Use a dollar sign and a decimal point to write one dollar. Use a cent sign to write amounts less than one dollar.

Write the value of the coins.
Circle the sets of coins that equal one dollar.

1.

$1.00

2.

_____

3.

_____

4.

_____

5.

_____

6.

_____

Go on

Name_____

Find the value of the coins.
Circle the correct answer.

 Remember
$100¢ = \$1.00$

7.

less than $\$1.00$

equal to $\$1.00$

8.

less than $\$1.00$

equal to $\$1.00$

9.

less than $\$1.00$

equal to $\$1.00$

10.

less than $\$1.00$

equal to $\$1.00$

Problem Solving ▶ Reasoning

11. Tara has 2 quarters and 6 dimes. Does she have more than $\$1.00$ or less than $\$1.00$?

Draw or write to explain.

more than $\$1.00$ less than $\$1.00$

 At Home Show your child groups of coins that are equal to and less than $\$1.00$. Ask your child to find the value of the coins.

Chapter 14   three hundred ninety-three **393**

Now Try This   Dollars and Cents

Write dollars and cents for amounts greater than $1.00.

one dollar and thirty cents

$1.30
↑ ↑
dollars cents

one dollar and three cents

$1.03
↑ ↑
dollars cents

Write the value of the coins in dollars and cents.
Circle the group of coins that has a greater value.

1.

_____   _____

2.

_____   _____

Equal Amounts

MathTracks 2/12
Listen and Understand

Different sets of coins can make **equal amounts.**

Objective
Show equal amounts with different coin combinations.

Vocabulary
equal amount

25¢   25¢   25¢

Guided Practice

Use coins.
Show two ways to make 50¢.
Draw the coins.

Think
I can show 50¢ with quarters, dimes, nickels and pennies.

1. 50¢

2. 50¢

TEST TIPS **Explain Your Thinking** Would it take more nickels or dimes to make 50¢? How do you know?

Use coins.
Show two ways to make this amount.
Draw the coins.

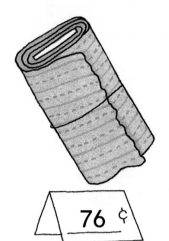

76 ¢

1. 76¢

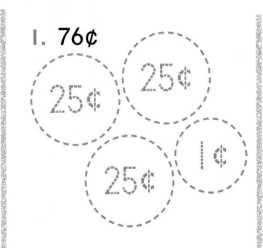

2. 76¢

97 ¢

3. 97¢

4. 97¢

Problem Solving ▶ **Number Sense**

5. Deena has 22¢. She has only
1 nickel. Draw the coins she
could have.

Draw or write to explain.

 At Home Give your child several quarters, dimes, and nickels.
Ask him or her to show 45¢ two ways. Repeat with other amounts.

Name_____

Make a List

Objective
Make a list to solve a problem.

You can make a list to help you solve a problem.

Jo Ann wants to buy a top.
She has quarters, dimes, and nickels.
How many ways can she make 35¢?

UNDERSTAND

What do you know?

- Jo Ann wants a top.
- A top costs 35¢.
- Jo Ann has quarters, dimes, and nickels.

PLAN

Use coins to make a list.
Find ways to make the money amount.

SOLVE

Complete the list.

Make 35¢

25¢	10¢	5¢
		2

There are ___6___ ways to make 35¢ with quarters, dimes, and nickels.

LOOK BACK

Did you answer the question?
How do you know you found all the ways?

Guided Practice

Use coins to solve.
Complete the list.

1. Lisa wants a doll. She has dimes and nickels. How many ways can she make 25¢?

   Think
   2 dimes and 1 nickel is one way.

   Lisa can make 25¢ _____ ways.

Make 25¢	
10¢	5¢
2	1

Practice

2. Mario wants a book. He has quarters, dimes, and nickels. Show four ways he can make 30¢.

   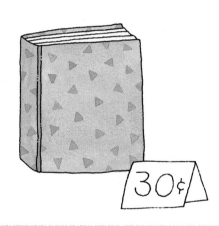

Make 30¢		
25¢	10¢	5¢

3. Megi wants a toy car. She has quarters, dimes, and nickels. Show five ways she can make 40¢.

   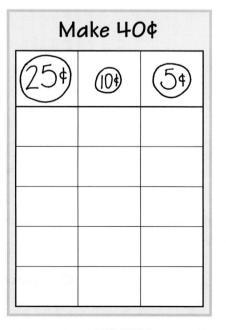

Make 40¢		
25¢	10¢	5¢

Go on ➡

Name _____

Strategies

Make a List
Guess and Check
Write a Number Sentence

Choose a Strategy

Solve.

1. Luc wants to buy a checkerboard for 20¢. He has dimes and nickels. Show the three ways he can make 20¢.

Draw or write to explain.

Make 20¢	
 (10¢)	(5¢)

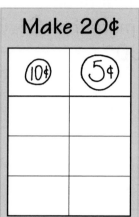
checkerboard

2. Marbles come in these bags. Emilia wants to buy 40 marbles. Which two bags should she buy?

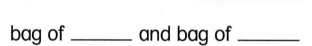
marbles

bag of _____ and bag of _____

3. Paul buys 15 kumquats. He shares 7 of the kumquats with his friends. How many kumquats does Paul have left?

_____ kumquats

kumquats

4. **Multistep** Inez has 9 pink carnations and 7 yellow carnations. She uses 10 carnations for her mother's hat. How many carnations does Inez have left?

_____ carnations

carnations

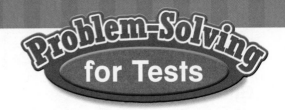

Problem-Solving for Tests

Listening Skills

TEST PREP

Listen to your teacher read the problem.
Solve.

1. Paulo has 3 quarters and 3 dimes. Does he have more than $1.00 or less than $1.00?

Show your work using pictures, numbers, or words.

_____________ than $1.00

2. Mr. Doria took 24 pictures at recess. He took another 48 pictures during gym. How many pictures did Mr. Doria take?

______ pictures

Listen to your teacher read the problem.
Choose the correct answer.

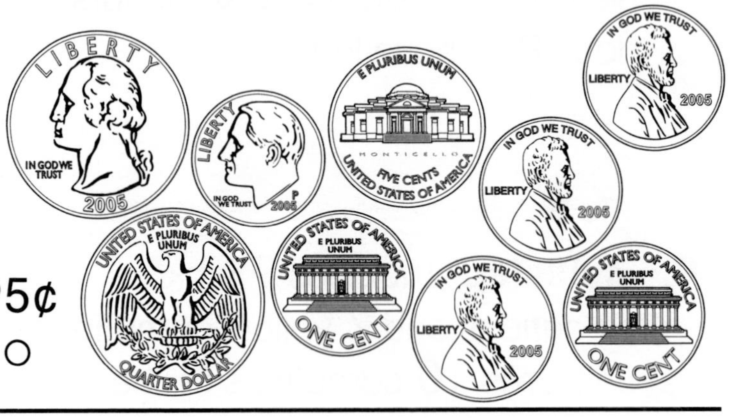

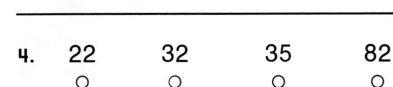

3. 65¢ ○ 70¢ ○ 75¢ ○ 95¢ ○

4. 22 ○ 32 ○ 35 ○ 82 ○

Quick Check

Find the value of the coins.
Circle the correct answer.

1.

less than $1.00

equal to $1.00

2.

less than $1.00

equal to $1.00

Write the value of the coins in dollars and cents.

3.

$_____._____

Show two ways to make the amount.
Draw the coins.

4. 41¢   41¢

Make a list to solve.

5. Pat wants to buy a toy that costs 19¢.
   He has dimes, nickels, and pennies.
   Show three ways he can make 19¢.

Make 19¢		
10¢	5¢	1¢

Add.

1. 65
    +20

2. 40
    +19

3. 38
    + 5

4. 57
    + 8

5. 22
    + 5

6. 43
    +27

7. 24
    +39

8. 76
    +18

9. 35
    +64

10. 58
    +34

Subtract.

11. 47
    −20

12. 78
    −30

13. 52
    − 4

14. 69
    − 7

15. 83
    − 5

16. 63
    −17

17. 57
    −28

18. 46
    −16

19. 95
    −64

20. 68
    −29

Social Studies Connection

Pesos

In the United States, 1 dollar equals 100 cents. In Mexico, 1 peso equals 100 centavos.

Think
Count by hundreds.

How many centavos are in 3 pesos? _____

How many centavos are in 5 pesos? _____

WEEKLY WR READER eduplace.com/kids/mw/

402 four hundred two

Name_____

Vocabulary (*e • Glossary*)

Choose a word to complete the sentence.

| nickel |
| quarter |
| cent sign |

1. A _____ has a value of 25¢.

2. When you write 5 cents you use a 5 and a _____.

Concepts and Skills

Count on to find the value of the coins.

3.

_____¢ _____¢ _____¢ _____¢ _____¢   ⎕⎕

Write the value of the coins in dollars and cents.

4.

_____¢

5.

_____¢

6.

_____

Find the value of the coins.
Circle the correct answer.

7.

less than $1.00

equal to $1.00

8.

less than $1.00

greater than $1.00

Use coins.
Show two ways to make the amount.
Draw the coins.

9. 76¢

76¢

Problem Solving

Use coins to solve.
Complete the list.

10. Tess needs 45¢ for the bus. She has quarters, dimes, and nickels. Show five ways she can make 45¢.

Make 45¢		
25¢	10¢	5¢

CHAPTER 15

Using Money

INVESTIGATION

What things can you buy with 50¢?

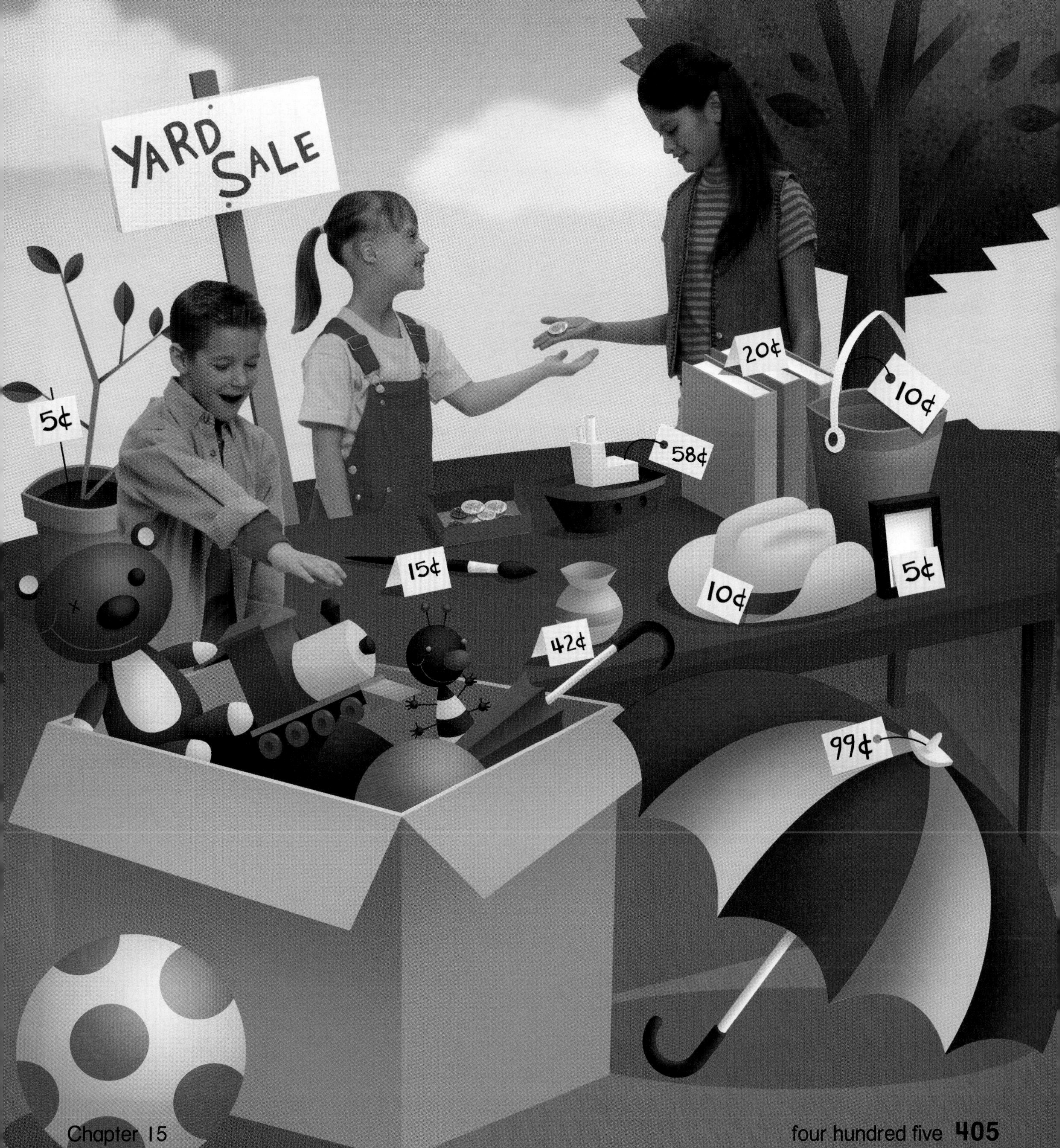
YARD SALE
5¢
20¢
10¢
58¢
15¢
10¢
5¢
42¢
99¢

People Using Math

Sacajawea

Sacajawea lived about **200** years ago. She was a brave and strong woman. She helped two explorers, Lewis and Clark, find their way to the Pacific Ocean. Their group traveled across the Northwest of our country. In **1806** they made it to the "great sea," the Pacific Ocean.

The United States honored her in 2000 by putting a picture of Sacajawea and her baby on a coin worth $1.00 (100 cents).

Solve.

Draw or write to explain.

1. How many quarters would you need to trade for a dollar coin?

_____ quarters

2. How many dimes would you need to trade for a dollar coin?

_____ dimes

3. How many nickels would you need to trade for a dollar coin?

_____ nickels

4. How many pennies would you need to trade for a dollar coin?

_____ pennies

Make an Exact Amount

Objective
Use coins to show an
exact amount of money.

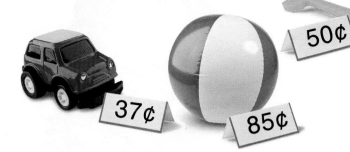

37¢   50¢   85¢   70¢

Ana wants to buy the car.
She chooses the coins to
make the exact amount.

Luis wants to buy the hat.
He needs more coins to
make the exact amount.

Count: 25¢, 35¢, 36¢, 37¢

Count: 25¢, 35¢, 45¢, 55¢, 60¢
Luis needs 10¢ more.

Guided Practice

Circle the coins that make the exact amount.

1.

Think
I start counting
with the quarter.

50¢

2.

65¢

TEST TIPS **Explain Your Thinking** Are 3 quarters and 3 pennies
enough to pay for a toy that costs 83¢? How do you know?

Circle the coins that make the exact amount.

1.

63¢

2.

46¢

3.

85¢

Problem Solving ▶ Reasoning

Draw or write to explain.

4. You buy the hat. Show how to pay the exact amount with three coins.

5. Talk About It Did everyone show the same coins? Why?

55¢

At Home Ask your child to use coins to show you amounts of money between 10¢ and 99¢.

Compare Money Values

MathTracks 2/13
Listen and Understand

Compare the values of two sets of coins.

Objective
Compare the values of groups of money.

Vocabulary
greater than (>)
less than (<)
equal (=)

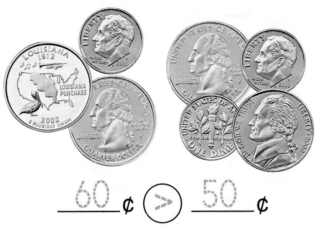

___60___¢ (>) ___50___¢

60¢ is **greater than** 50¢.

___30___¢ (<) ___65___¢

30¢ is **less than** 65¢.

Guided Practice

Write the value of the sets of coins. Compare the sets. Write >, <, or =.

Think
When the values are the same use an **=** .

1.

___56___¢ ( ) ___56___¢

2.

_____¢ ( ) _____¢

TEST TIPS **Explain Your Thinking** Do 5 coins always have a greater value than 3 coins? How do you know?

Write the value of the sets of coins.
Compare the sets.

1.

___42___ ¢ ⊙(>) ___26___ ¢

2.

$_____ ◯ _____ ¢

3.

_____ ¢ ◯ _____ ¢

4.

_____ ¢ ◯ _____ ¢

Problem Solving ▶ Reasoning

Draw or write to explain.

5. Maria does not have enough money
to buy this bag. She needs 10¢
more. How much money
does Maria have?

$1.00

_____ ¢

 At Home Ask your child to count the value of two unequal
groups of coins and tell which group has the greater value.

Name _____

Use the Fewest Coins

MathTracks 2/14
Listen and Understand

Josh pays for the book
with the fewest coins.
What coins does he use?

A half-dollar
has the greatest
value but it is more
than 40¢.

Objective
Use the fewest
coins to show an
amount of money.

Hands-On

Step 1

Find the coin of the greatest value.
Try a quarter.

___25___ ¢

Step 2

Count on until you reach 40¢.

___35___ ¢   ___40___ ¢

Josh uses a ___quarter___, a ___dime___, and a ___nickel___.

Guided Practice

Find the fewest coins that show the amount.
Draw the coins.

1.

    Ten Little Puppies

    56¢

    Think
    Which coin
    should I start with
    to show 56¢?

2.

    Feathers for Lunch

    19¢

3.

    38¢

TEST TIPS **Explain Your Thinking** How do you decide which coin you
can start with to use the fewest coins?

Find the fewest coins that show the amount.
Draw the coins.

Start with the coin of greatest value and count on.

1.

75¢

2.

81¢

3.

79¢

4.

87¢

Problem Solving ▶ Data Sense

Find the fewest coins that show the amount.
Complete the table to show how many of each coin are needed.

		Half-dollar	Quarter	Dime	Nickel	Penny
5.	29¢					
6.	82¢					

At Home Have your child use the fewest coins
to show 16¢, 32¢, 58¢, 95¢, and $1.00.

Name_____

Compare Prices and Amounts

Do you have enough money to buy the glasses?

69¢

Compare. 70¢ is more than 69¢.

Yes. You have enough money.

Guided Practice

Write the amount.
Is there enough money?
Circle **Yes** or **No**.

Think
I start counting with the coin of the greatest value.

1. 50¢ _____ ¢

   Yes   No

2. 36¢ _____ ¢

   Yes   No

3. 85¢ _____ ¢

   Yes   No

TEST TIPS **Explain Your Thinking** Could you buy the pail in Exercise 1 if you had another nickel? Why?

Write the amount of money.
Is there enough money? Circle **Yes** or **No**.

Remember to compare the price to the value of the coins.

1.

26¢

2̶7̶ ¢

(Yes)   No

2.

42¢

_____ ¢

Yes   No

3.

75¢

_____ ¢

Yes   No

4.

51¢

_____ ¢

Yes   No

Problem Solving ▶ Reasoning

5. Flora wants to buy the toy.
   Does she have enough money?

Draw or write to explain.

$1.19

Yes   No

At Home Give your child some coins and a grocery flyer. Ask him or her if they have enough money to buy each item that is less than $1.00.

Go on ▶

Name_____

Now Try This   Estimating Costs

You have these coins. Do you have
enough money to buy this hat?

I know that
3 quarters is more
than 50¢. I have
enough money.

Sometimes, you do not need to count.
You can estimate.

Can you buy the item?
Estimate the amount of money.
Circle **Yes** or **No**.

1.  95¢       Yes   No

2.  18¢      Yes   No

3.  56¢        Yes   No

4.  85¢        Yes   No

5.  20¢      Yes   No

Quick Check

Circle the coins that make the exact amount.

1.  42¢

Write the value of the sets of coins.

Compare the sets. Write >, <, or =.

2.

_____ ¢ ◯ _____ ¢

Find the fewest coins that show the amount.
Draw the coins.

3. 68¢

Write the amount. Is there enough money?
Circle **Yes** or **No**.

_____ ¢

4.  48¢

Yes   No

Can you buy the item? Estimate.
Circle **Yes** or **No**.

5.  38¢

Yes   No

Add and Subtract Amounts of Money

You add and subtract money the same way you add and subtract two-digit numbers.

$$\begin{array}{r} 15 \\ +15 \\ \hline 30 \end{array} \qquad \begin{array}{r} 15¢ \\ +15¢ \\ \hline 30¢ \end{array} \qquad \begin{array}{r} \overset{4\;10}{5\cancel{0}} \\ -15 \\ \hline 35 \end{array} \qquad \begin{array}{r} \overset{4\;10}{5\cancel{0}}¢ \\ -15¢ \\ \hline 35¢ \end{array}$$

Guided Practice

Add or subtract.

1. $\begin{array}{r} 52¢ \\ -18¢ \\ \hline \end{array}$

Think
52¢ − 18¢
is like
52 − 18.

2. $\begin{array}{r} 17¢ \\ +8¢ \\ \hline \end{array}$

3. $\begin{array}{r} 74¢ \\ -28¢ \\ \hline \end{array}$

4. $\begin{array}{r} 43¢ \\ -36¢ \\ \hline \end{array}$

Rewrite the numbers.
Then add or subtract.

5. 33¢ + 48¢

$$\begin{array}{r} 3\,|\,3\,¢ \\ +4\,|\,8\,¢ \\ \hline 8\,|\,1\,¢ \end{array}$$

6. 96¢ − 8¢

7. 47¢ − 19¢

8. 56¢ + 13¢

TEST TIPS **Explain Your Thinking** How is adding money different from adding numbers?

Remember
Write the ¢ sign in your answer.

SEEDS 95¢

Add or subtract.

1.
$$\begin{array}{r} {}^{6}\,{}^{10} \\ 7\cancel{0}¢ \\ -18¢ \\ \hline 52¢ \end{array}$$

2.
$$\begin{array}{r} 26¢ \\ +48¢ \\ \hline \end{array}$$

3.
$$\begin{array}{r} 32¢ \\ +40¢ \\ \hline \end{array}$$

4.
$$\begin{array}{r} 78¢ \\ -\ \ 9¢ \\ \hline \end{array}$$

5.
$$\begin{array}{r} 67¢ \\ -48¢ \\ \hline \end{array}$$

6.
$$\begin{array}{r} 59¢ \\ -34¢ \\ \hline \end{array}$$

7.
$$\begin{array}{r} 47¢ \\ +\ \ 5¢ \\ \hline \end{array}$$

8.
$$\begin{array}{r} 50¢ \\ +28¢ \\ \hline \end{array}$$

9.
$$\begin{array}{r} 34¢ \\ -19¢ \\ \hline \end{array}$$

10.
$$\begin{array}{r} 58¢ \\ -37¢ \\ \hline \end{array}$$

Rewrite the numbers.

Then add or subtract.

11. 90¢ − 75¢

12. 57¢ + 12¢

13. 85¢ − 66¢

14. 27¢ + 6¢

$$\begin{array}{r} {}^{8}\quad{}^{10} \\ 9\ \ \cancel{0}¢ \\ -\ 7\ \ 5¢ \\ \hline 1\ \ 5¢ \end{array}$$

Problem Solving ▶ Reasoning

SEED

50¢   23¢

15. You have 9 dimes. You buy the bird seed and bird house. How much money do you have left?

Draw or write to explain.

_____ ¢

At Home Give your child a few coins. Ask him or her if there is enough money to buy either of the items shown above.

Make Change With Pennies and Nickels

 MathTracks 2/15
Listen and Understand

Objective
Count on to make change with pennies and nickels.

Vocabulary
change

When you pay more money than the price you get **change.**

Beth buys:

She pays:

Make change.
Count on from the price
to the amount given.

43¢

50¢

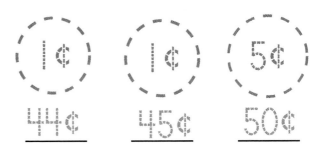

(1¢) (1¢) (5¢)

44¢   45¢   50¢

The change is ___7¢___.

Guided Practice

Write the amount paid.
Draw coins and count on to find the change.

Think
I can count on from
17¢ to 20¢.

Amount Paid	Price	Draw Coins to Count On	Change
1. ____ ¢	17¢	____ ¢ ____ ¢ ____ ¢	____ ¢
2. ____ ¢	19¢	____ ¢ ____ ¢	____ ¢

TEST TIPS **Explain Your Thinking** Why do you start with the penny in Exercise 2?

Count on with pennies and nickels to find the change.

Write the amount paid.
Draw coins and count on to find the change.

	Amount Paid	Price	Draw Coins to Count On	Change
1.	_____ ¢	32¢	1¢ 1¢ 1¢ ___¢ ___¢ ___¢	_____ ¢
2.	_____ ¢	43¢	___¢ ___¢ ___¢	_____ ¢
3.	_____ ¢	60¢	___¢ ___¢ ___¢	_____ ¢
4.	$___.___	89¢	___¢ ___¢ $___.___	_____ ¢

Problem Solving ▶ Reasoning

5. Jamie pays for this puppet with 3 quarters. How much change will he get?

71¢

Draw or write to explain.

_____ ¢

At Home Play store with your child. Take turns counting out change with pennies and nickels.

Make Change With Nickels, Dimes, and Quarters

70¢

Omar buys a flashlight for 70¢.
He pays with a dollar bill.
How much change does he get?

Omar pays:

The clerk makes change.
She counts on from the price
to the amount given.

The price is 70¢.

$1.00   75¢ $1.00   Omar gets ___30¢___ in change.

Guided Practice

Write the amount paid.
Count on from the price to find the change.

Think
Count on from
10¢ to 50¢.

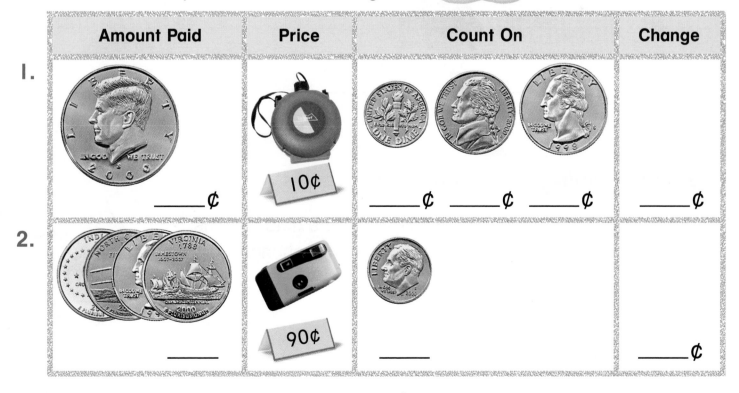

	Amount Paid	Price	Count On	Change
1.	_____ ¢	10¢	_____ ¢ _____ ¢ _____ ¢	_____ ¢
2.	_____	90¢	_____	_____ ¢

TEST TIPS **Explain Your Thinking** You have $1.00. Will you get more change if you buy something for 89¢ or for 29¢? How do you know?

Count the coins to find the amount of change.

Write the amount paid.
Draw the coins and count on to find the change.

	Amount Paid	Price	Count On			Change
1.	$1.00	What Will the Weather Be Like Today? 60¢	10¢ 70¢	5¢ 75¢	25¢ $1.00	40¢
2.	_____¢	15¢	_____¢	_____¢		_____¢
3.	_____¢	55¢	_____¢	_____¢		_____¢

Problem Solving ▶ Reasoning

4. Vera pays for this map with a dollar bill. She gets 4 coins for change. What coins did she get back for change?

Draw or write to explain.

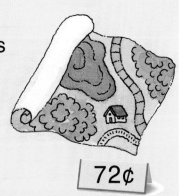

72¢

At Home Have your child name other coins that could have been given as change for Exercises 1–3.

Act It Out With Models

Tom has 4 dimes, 2 nickels, and 2 pennies. Does he have enough money to buy the toy?

Objective
Use models to act out and solve problems.

55¢

UNDERSTAND

What do you know?
· Tom has some money.
· The toy costs 55¢.

PLAN

Act out the problem to solve.
Use coins to show Tom's money.
Find the total amount.

Tom has __52¢__ .

SOLVE

Compare the amount of money Tom has to the price of the toy.
Tom has 52¢. The toy costs __55¢__ .

52¢ $\bigcirc{<}$ 55¢

Does Tom have enough money to buy the toy? __No__

LOOK BACK

Does your answer make sense?
What helped you decide if Tom could buy the toy?

Remember:
► Understand
► Plan
► Solve
► Look Back

Guided Practice

Use coins to act out the problem. Solve.

1. Ramon has 1 quarter and 3 dimes. His mother gives him another dime. How much money does he have?

Draw or write to explain.

Think
I can count on: 25, 35, 45, 55. He starts with 55¢.

_____

2. Ron has 1 quarter and 1 dime. He wants to buy a puzzle for 30¢. Does he have enough money?

Think
I need to compare money amounts.

_____

Practice

3. Sara has 2 quarters, 1 nickel, and 1 penny. How much more money does she need to buy a jump rope for 78¢?

_____

4. **Multistep** Tami earns 25¢ to set the table and 10¢ to walk the dog. If she does each job 2 times, how much will she earn?

_____

Go on

Name_____

Choose a Strategy

Solve.

Draw or write to explain.

1. Paula has 2 quarters, 1 dime, and 3 nickels. This is the same amount as the price of a Mazahua doll. How much is the doll?

Mazahua doll

_____¢

2. Bob has 3 quarters and 1 dime. He wants to buy a Kachina doll. It costs 82¢. Does Bob have enough money to buy a Kachina doll?

Kachina doll

_____

3. Kareem is saving for a Matryoshka. He has 3 quarters and a dime. This is the same as the price of a Matryoshka. How much is the doll?

Matryoshka doll

_____¢

4. **Multistep** Anne wants to buy two Gosho dolls. Each doll is 45¢. She has 2 quarters and 2 nickels. How much more does she need?

Gosho doll

_____¢

At Home Give your child one quarter and several dimes and nickels. Ask if there is enough to buy items that cost 60¢, 75¢, 80¢, and 95¢.

Listening Skills

Listen to your teacher read the problem.
Solve.

1. Beth has a coin album. Each page holds 5 coins. The coins on the first page have a total value of 25¢. What 5 coins are on page 1?

Show your work using pictures, numbers, or words.

5 _____

2. Tim has 1 quarter, 2 pennies, and 1 other coin. He has a total of 37¢. What is the other coin?

_____

Listen to your teacher read the problem.
Choose the correct answer.

3.

○   ○   ○   ○

4.   51¢   46¢   41¢   15¢
      ○   ○   ○   ○

Name _____

Quick Check

Write the amount paid.
Count on from the price to find the change.

Amount Paid	Price	Draw Coins to Count On	Change
1. _____	  33¢	_____ _____ _____	_____
2. _____	  60¢	_____ _____ _____	_____

Add or subtract.

3. 67¢
  −24¢
  _____

4. 36¢
  +28¢
  _____

5. 59¢
  +32¢
  _____

6. 78¢
  −49¢
  _____

7. 90¢
  −75¢
  _____

Use coins to act out the problem.
Solve.

Draw or write to explain.

8. Marty has 1 quarter and 2 nickels.
He wants to buy a notebook that
costs 34¢. Does he have enough
money?

_____

Chapter 15

four hundred twenty-seven **427**

Write the fraction for the shaded parts.

1. 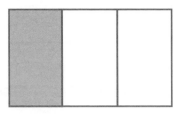 _____

2. 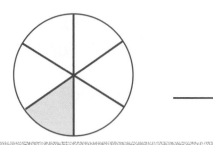 _____

3. 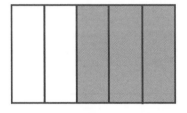 _____

4. 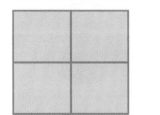 _____

5.  _____

6. 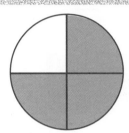 _____

7. 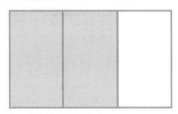 _____

8. 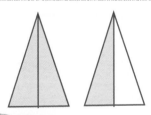 _____

Social Studies Connection

Lost and Found Coins

Spanish coins were found on a ship that sank in 1622. The coins were Pieces of Eight. One Piece of Eight had the same value as 8 Reales, a Spanish coin of less value.

Complete the table to find how many Reales have the same value as the Pieces of Eight.

Pieces of Eight	1	2	3	4
Reales	8			

Name_____

Vocabulary (*e* • Glossary)

Use the words in a sentence.

| greater than |
| less than |

1. _____

_____

2. _____

_____

Concepts and Skills

Circle the coins that make the exact amount.

3.

49¢

4. Write the value of the sets of coins. Compare the sets.

Write >, <, or =.

 _____ ◯ _____

Find the fewest coins that show the amount.
Draw the coins.

5.

47¢

Write the amount.
Is there enough money?
Circle **Yes** or **No**.

6.

_____ ¢

Yes   No

Add or subtract.

7. 48¢
   +43¢

8. 67¢
   −18¢

Write the amount paid.
Draw the coins and count on to find the change.

Amount Paid	Price	Draw Coins to Count On	Change
 9.	 35¢		
_____ ¢		_____ ¢ _____ ¢	_____ ¢

Problem Solving

Use coins to act out the problem.
Solve.

10. Annika has 1 quarter and 1 penny.
    She wants to buy a pen that costs 23¢.
    Does she have enough money?

Draw or write to explain.

_____

Time and Calendar

INVESTIGATION

How do you know when it is morning or night?

Telling Time

Draw a picture of something you do at this time of day.

Name_____

Activity: Estimate Time

There are 60 **seconds** in a **minute**.

1 minute ⟶

Objective
Understand and estimate lengths of time.

Vocabulary
seconds
minute

It takes about one second to raise my hand.

Estimate the length of a minute.

• Close your eyes.
• Your teacher will tell you when the minute starts.
• Raise your hand when you think one minute has passed.

Work Together

Estimate how many times you can do the activity in one minute.
Then do the activity for one minute.
Count the number of times you do it.

	Activity	Estimate	Count
1.	Say the alphabet.		
2.	Touch your toes.		
3.	Write your name.		
4.	Count to 25.		

5. **Talk About It** Which activity did you do the least number of times? Why do you think you did this the least?

It takes about one second to raise your hand.

It takes about one minute to count slowly from 1 to 60.

It takes about one hour to play a game of soccer.

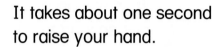

Think about the length of time.
Draw or write things you do that take that long.

1. About 5 seconds

2. About 5 minutes

3. About 1 hour

4. **Talk About It** Compare your drawings with your classmates. How are they alike or different?

At Home Help your child make a list of things he or she does during a typical day. Ask which takes seconds, minutes, or hours to do.

Time to the Hour and Half-Hour

There are **60** minutes in one **hour**.

In one hour the **minute hand** moves all the way around a clock.

60
0

9 o'clock

9:00

There are **30** minutes in a **half-hour**.

In a half-hour the minute hand moves halfway around a clock.

60
0

30 minutes after 9

hour → 9:30 ← minutes after the hour

Work Together

Write the time.

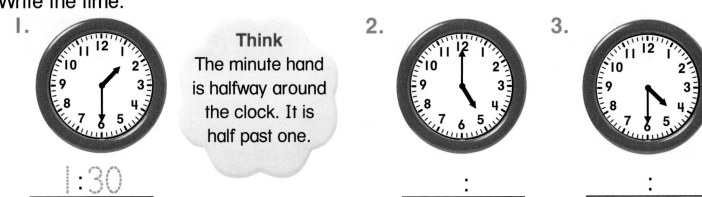

1.

Think
The minute hand is halfway around the clock. It is half past one.

1:30

2.

____:____

3.

____:____

Draw the minute hand to show the time.

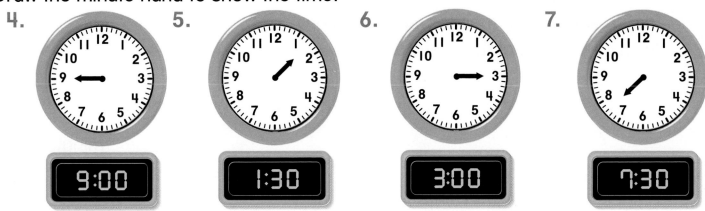

4.

9:00

5.

1:30

6.

3:00

7.

7:30

TEST TIPS **Explain Your Thinking** Where is the hour hand on the clock in Exercise 3? Why?

The minute hand points to 12 at the hour and 6 at the half-hour.

Write the time.

1.

8:00

2.

____ : ____

3.

____ : ____

Draw the minute hand to show the time.

4.

7:00

5.

6:00

6.

12:30

7.

9:30

Problem Solving ▶ Measurement Sense

8. Jamal goes to the playground. He swings for 30 minutes. He plays with his friends for a half-hour and then leaves. How many minutes is Jamal at the playground?

Draw or write to explain.

____ minutes

9. What is another way to write this amount of time?

____ hour

 At Home Ask your child to tell you the time at 6:30, 7:00, and 7:30.

Name_____

Time to Five Minutes

MathTracks 2/16
Listen and Understand

Skip count by 5s to count the minutes.

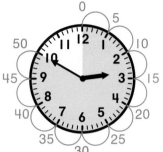

20 minutes after 2

hour → 2:20 ← minutes after the hour

50 minutes after 2

2:50

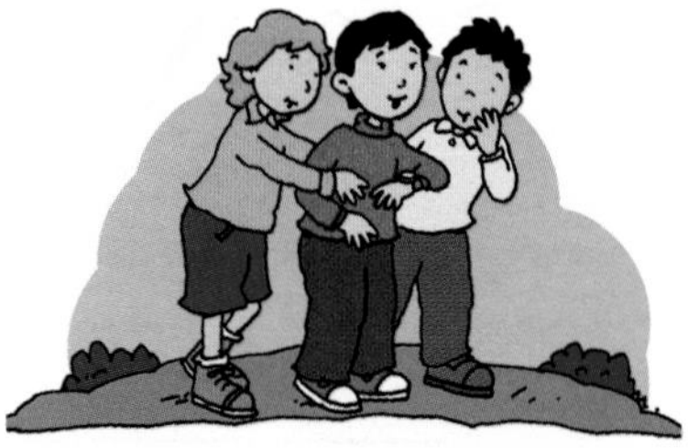

Guided Practice

Write the time.

1.

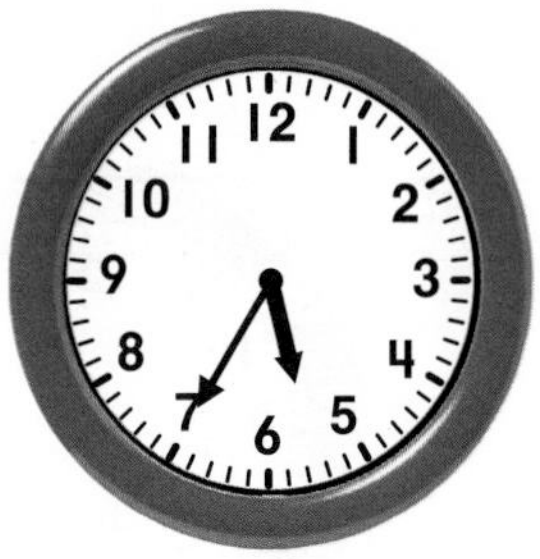

Think
Start at the 12.
Count 5, 10, 15, 20, 25, 30, 35.

____ : ____

2.

____ : ____

3.

____ : ____

Draw the minute hand to show the time.

4.

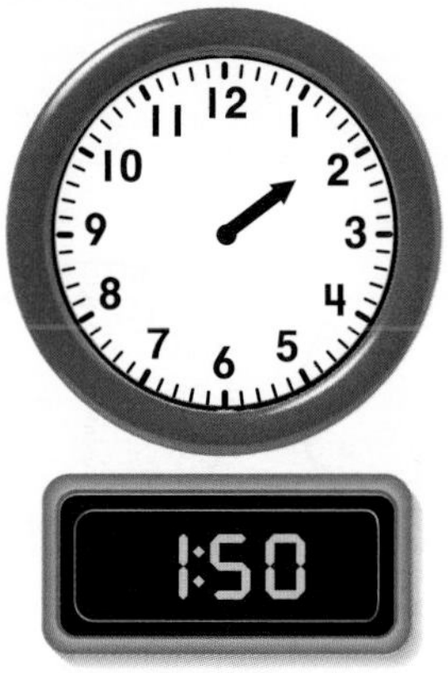

1:50

5.

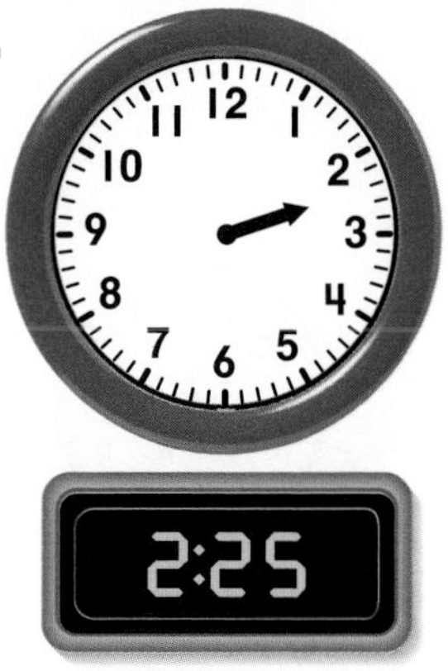

2:25

6.

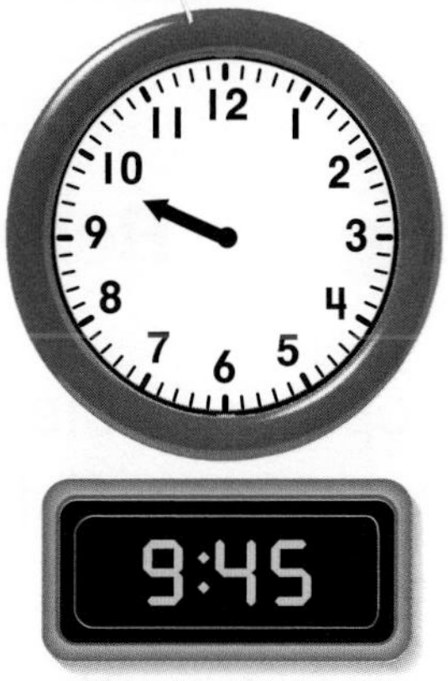

9:45

7.

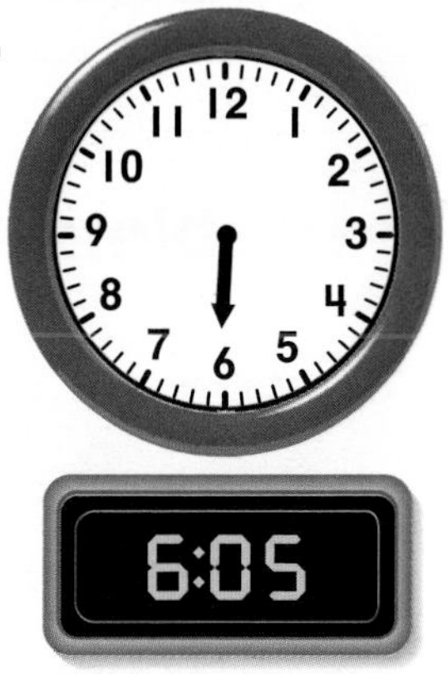

6:05

TEST TIPS **Explain Your Thinking** Why can you skip count by 5s to find the minutes after the hour?

Remember to start at the 12. Then skip count by 5s to find the minutes after the hour.

Write the time.

1.

4:55

2.

____:____

3.

____:____

4.

____:____

5.

____:____

6.

____:____

7.

____:____

8.

____:____

Draw the minute hand to show the time.

9.

9:00

10.

3:30

11.

2:45

12.

6:10

Problem Solving ▶ Reasoning

13. Sometimes people estimate time, and use the word about. Estimate these times to the nearest 5 minutes. Then draw a line to match.

about 5:30   about 5:45   about 5:15

At Home Have your child use the exercises on this page to show you how he or she counts by 5s to tell time.

Go on

Now Try This **Time to the Minute**

First count by 5s.
Then count on by 1s to
tell time to the minute.

Start at the 12.
I count 5, 10, 15,
then 16, 17, 18.

18 minutes after 8

8:18

Write the time.

1.

Think
I start at 12.
I count 5, 10, 15,
20, 25, 30,
31, 32.

____ : ____

2.

____ : ____

3.

____ : ____

4.

____ : ____

5.

____ : ____

6.

____ : ____

7.

____ : ____

Continue the pattern. Write the times that come next.

8.

9.

10. Write your own clock pattern. Ask a friend to continue it.

Play All Day

2 Players

What You Need: paper clip, pencil, and counter for each player

How to Play

1. Put counters on START TIME.

2. Take turns spinning the spinner. Move forward the amount of time you spin.

3. Continue taking turns until one player reaches 4:00.

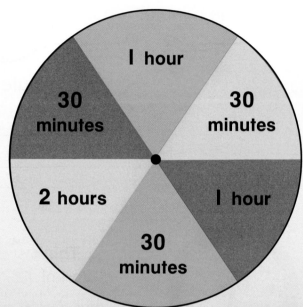

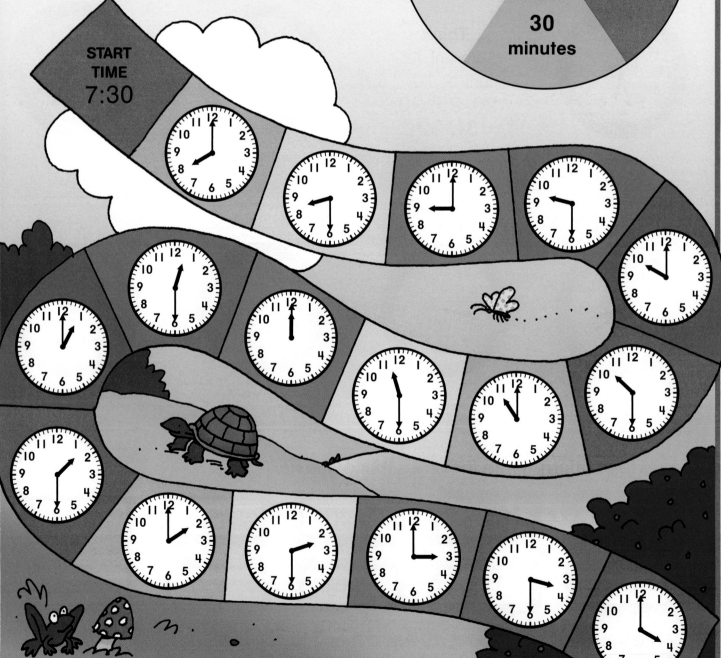

Time to 15 Minutes

MathTracks 2/17
Listen and Understand

Objective
Tell time to the quarter-hour.

Vocabulary
quarter-hour

There are 15 minutes in a **quarter-hour.**

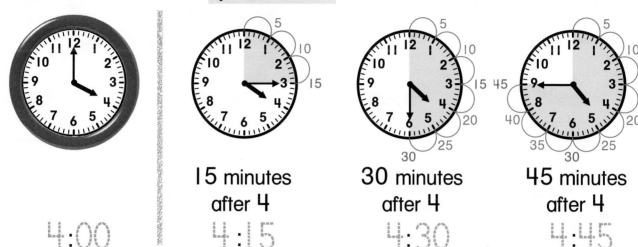

4:00

15 minutes
after 4

4:15

30 minutes
after 4

4:30

45 minutes
after 4

4:45

In a quarter-hour the minute hand moves around
one fourth of the clock.

Guided Practice

Write the time.

1.

Think
The minute hand
is a quarter of the
way around the clock.
It is a quarter
past two.

_____:_____

2.

_____:_____

3.

_____:_____

Draw the minute hand to show the time.

4.

`11:00`

5.

`10:30`

6.

`10:45`

7.

`10:15`

TEST TIPS **Explain Your Thinking** How many quarter-hours are in 1 hour?
Tell or show how you know.

A quarter-hour is 15 minutes.

Write the time.

1.

9:15

2.

_____ : _____

3.

_____ : _____

4.

_____ : _____

5.

_____ : _____

6.

_____ : _____

7.

_____ : _____

8.

_____ : _____

Draw the minute hand to show the time.

9.

`8:00`

10.

`7:30`

11.

`10:15`

12.

`12:45`

Reading Math ▶ Vocabulary

Write the word that completes the sentence.

quarter-hour

half-hour

hour

13. An _____ is 60 minutes.

14. There are 15 minutes in a _____.

15. A _____ is the same as 30 minutes.

At Home Discuss things your child does every day that take about 15 minutes, such as making lunch.

Name ________________________________

WRITING MATH: CREATE AND SOLVE

Write the numbers on the clock.
Choose a time to show on
the clock. Draw hands
to show the time.

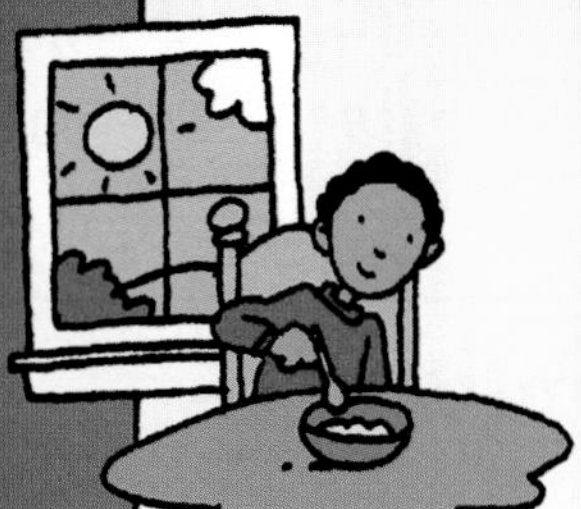

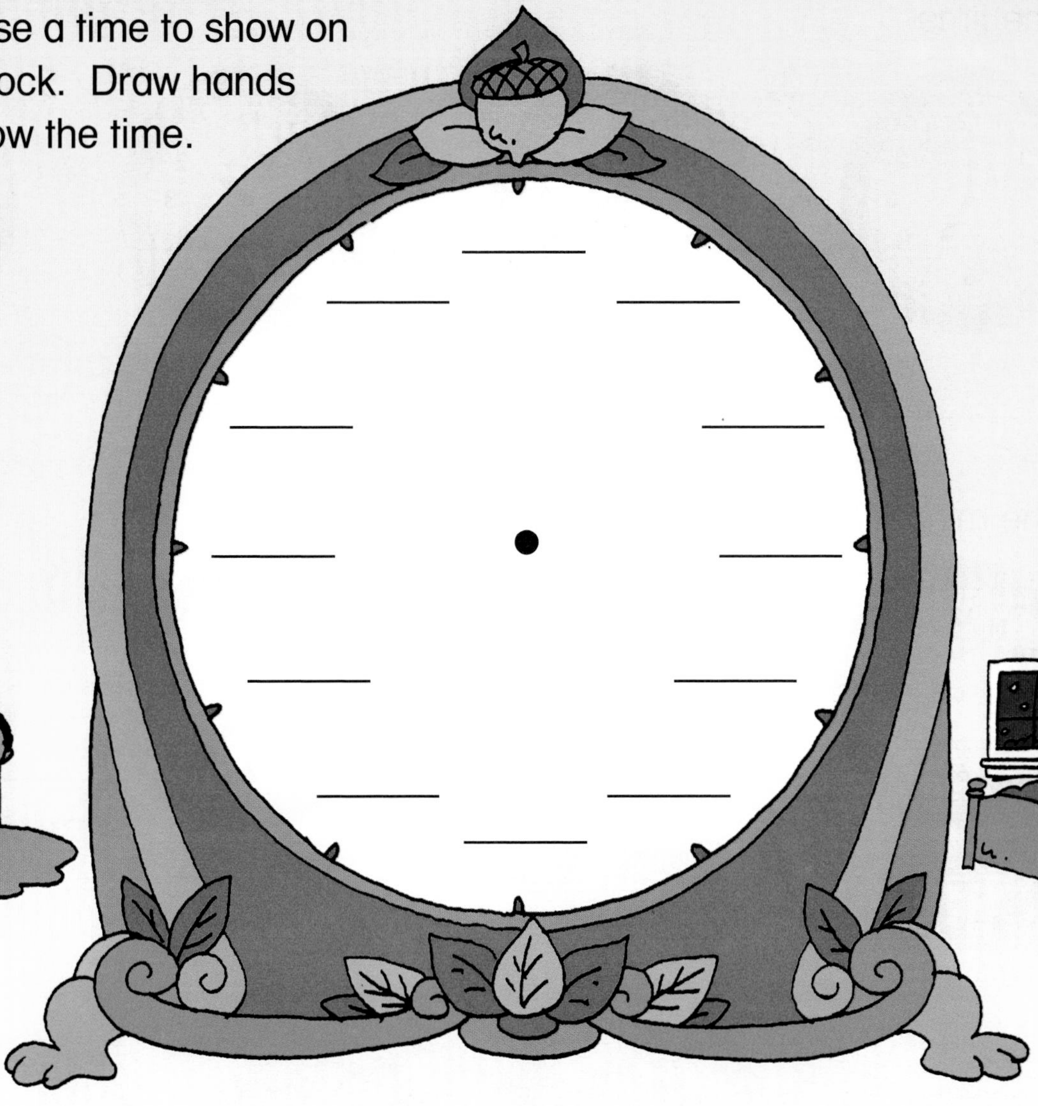

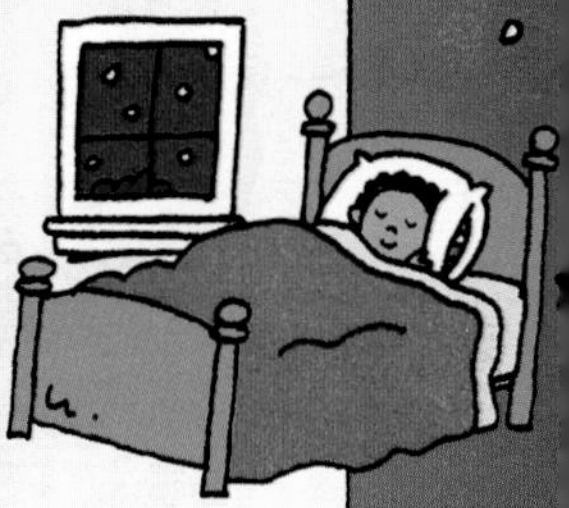

Write a problem that can be solved by using the clock.

____

____

____

____

____

Quick Check

1. Put an X on the activity that takes about one hour.

   Play a board game   Go on a field trip   Put on your shoes

Write the time.

2.

   _____ : _____

3.

   _____ : _____

4.

   _____ : _____

5.

   _____ : _____

Draw the minute hand to show the time.

6.

   3:30

7.

   6:45

8.

   5:10

9.

   12:35

Science Connection   Earth

Earth is always turning. Part of Earth is always facing the Sun. Part of Earth is always facing away from the Sun. It takes 24 hours for Earth to make one complete turn.

How many times does the hour hand go all the way around the clock in 24 hours?

_____ times

WEEKLY WR **READER** eduplace.com/kids/mw/

Name_____

Elapsed Time

 MathTracks 2/18
Listen and Understand

Objective
Determine how much time has passed.

Toys are on sale from
11:00 A.M. to 2:00 P.M.
How long does the toy sale last?

Counting on a clock can help you find how much time has passed.

P.M. is used for the time from 12 noon to 12 midnight.

A.M. is used for the time from 12 midnight to 12 noon.

Step 1

Begin at the start time.

Sale starts at 11:00 A.M.

Step 2

Count on each hour to the end time.

Sale ends at 2:00 P.M.

The sale lasts for ___3___ hours.

Guided Practice

Write the times.
Then write how much time has passed.

Think
4:00 to 5:00 is 1 hour,
5:00 to 6:00 is another hour.

1.

Start

End

_____:_____ P.M.   _____:_____ P.M.

The sale lasts for _____ hours.

2.

Start

End

_____:_____ A.M.   _____:_____ A.M.

The sale lasts for _____ hours.

TEST TIPS **Explain Your Thinking** How much time passes from 8:00 A.M. to 8:00 P.M.? Tell how you find the answer.

Remember to begin counting at the start time.

Write the times.
Then write how much time has passed.

	On Sale	Start Time	End Time	How long does the sale last?
1.		_8:00_ A.M.	_9:00_ A.M.	____ hour
2.	FRESH FRUIT	___:___ A.M.	___:___ P.M.	____ hours
3.		___:___ P.M.	___:___ P.M.	____ hours

Problem Solving ▶ Measurement Sense

Solve.

Draw or write to explain.

4. Gwen goes shopping at 10:00 A.M. She shops for 2 hours. What time does she finish?

5. **Talk About It** Is Gwen's finish time A.M. or P.M.? How do you know?

_____

At Home Have your child write the times he or she eats dinner and goes to sleep. Discuss how many hours pass between those times.

Name_____

Objective
Read and understand information in a calendar.

Vocabulary
calendar
day   week
month   year

Use a Calendar

A **calendar** shows **days** , **weeks** , and **months** in a **year** . This calendar shows one month.

April

Sunday	Monday	Tuesday	Wednesday	Thursday	Friday	Saturday
					1	2
3	4	5	6	7	8	9
10	11	12	13	14	15	16
17	18	19	20	21	22	23
24	25	26	27	28	29	30

Guided Practice

Use the calendar to answer the question.

> **Think**
> A row on the calendar shows one week.

1. How many days are in one week? _____

2. What day of the week is April 5? _____

3. What is the date of the first Monday? _____

4. What is the date of the third Tuesday? _____

5. How many Saturdays are there? _____

6. On what day of the week will the next month begin? _____

TEST TIPS **Explain Your Thinking** If you go to a piano lesson every 5 days, will you always go on the same day of the week? Why?

This calendar shows 1 year.
Use the calendar to answer the question.

A complete row of a calendar month shows one week or 7 days.

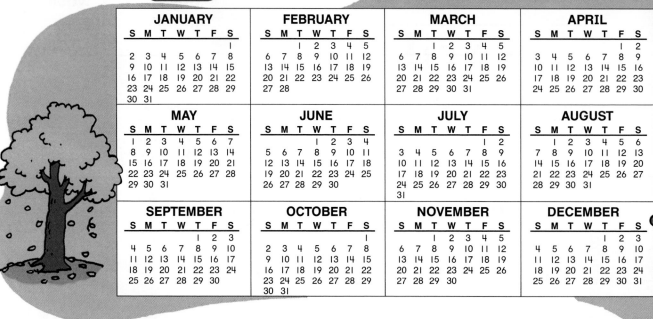

2005

JANUARY							FEBRUARY							MARCH							APRIL						
S	M	T	W	T	F	S	S	M	T	W	T	F	S	S	M	T	W	T	F	S	S	M	T	W	T	F	S
						1			1	2	3	4	5			1	2	3	4	5						1	2
2	3	4	5	6	7	8	6	7	8	9	10	11	12	6	7	8	9	10	11	12	3	4	5	6	7	8	9
9	10	11	12	13	14	15	13	14	15	16	17	18	19	13	14	15	16	17	18	19	10	11	12	13	14	15	16
16	17	18	19	20	21	22	20	21	22	23	24	25	26	20	21	22	23	24	25	26	17	18	19	20	21	22	23
23	24	25	26	27	28	29	27	28						27	28	29	30	31			24	25	26	27	28	29	30
30	31																										

MAY							JUNE							JULY							AUGUST						
S	M	T	W	T	F	S	S	M	T	W	T	F	S	S	M	T	W	T	F	S	S	M	T	W	T	F	S
1	2	3	4	5	6	7				1	2	3	4						1	2	1	2	3	4	5	6	
8	9	10	11	12	13	14	5	6	7	8	9	10	11	3	4	5	6	7	8	9	7	8	9	10	11	12	13
15	16	17	18	19	20	21	12	13	14	15	16	17	18	10	11	12	13	14	15	16	14	15	16	17	18	19	20
22	23	24	25	26	27	28	19	20	21	22	23	24	25	17	18	19	20	21	22	23	21	22	23	24	25	26	27
29	30	31					26	27	28	29	30			24	25	26	27	28	29	30	28	29	30	31			
														31													

SEPTEMBER							OCTOBER							NOVEMBER							DECEMBER						
S	M	T	W	T	F	S	S	M	T	W	T	F	S	S	M	T	W	T	F	S	S	M	T	W	T	F	S
				1	2	3							1			1	2	3	4	5					1	2	3
4	5	6	7	8	9	10	2	3	4	5	6	7	8	6	7	8	9	10	11	12	4	5	6	7	8	9	10
11	12	13	14	15	16	17	9	10	11	12	13	14	15	13	14	15	16	17	18	19	11	12	13	14	15	16	17
18	19	20	21	22	23	24	16	17	18	19	20	21	22	20	21	22	23	24	25	26	18	19	20	21	22	23	24
25	26	27	28	29	30		23	24	25	26	27	28	29	27	28	29	30				25	26	27	28	29	30	31
							30	31																			

1. What is the date one week after October 4? _October 11_

2. How many months are in one year? _____

3. Which is the twelfth month of the year? _____

4. What date follows May 31? _____

5. Which months have exactly 30 days? _____

_____

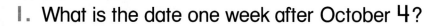

Algebra Readiness ▶ Patterns

Find the dates that come next in the pattern.

6. June 2   June 9   June 16

June ____   June ____

June 2005						
S	M	T	W	T	F	S
			1	2	3	4
5	6	7	8	9	10	11
12	13	14	15	16	17	18
19	20	21	22	23	24	25
26	27	28	29	30		

At Home Have your child use the calendar on this page to find his or her birthday. Ask what month comes before and what month comes after.

Name_____

Hours, Days, Weeks, and Months

Objective
Compare and estimate amounts of time.

Time is measured in different ways.
Which is longer, 2 weeks or 10 days?

SUN	MON	TUES	WED	THURS	FRI	SAT
1	2	3	4	5	6	7
8	9	10	11	12	13	14

24 hours = 1 day
7 days = 1 week
52 weeks = 1 year
12 months = 1 year

2 weeks is 14 days.
2 weeks is longer than 10 days.

Guided Practice

Circle the longer amount of time.

Think
I know that 1 day is 24 hours long.

1. 30 hours   1 day

2. 1 year   6 months

3. 45 weeks   1 year

Circle the shorter amount of time.

4. 1 week   10 days

5. 15 hours   1 day

6. 2 days   24 hours

7. 1 year   57 weeks

Use the words in the box. Write an estimate for the length of the activity.

hours	days	weeks	months

8. Swimming

9. Growing flowers

_____   _____

TEST TIPS **Explain Your Thinking** Is 2 weeks longer than 15 days?
How do you know?

Think about how long each activity takes.

Use the words in the box.
Write the best estimate for the length of the activity.

| hours | days | weeks | months |

1. Skating

___hours___

2. December school vacation

_____

3. Riding a bike

_____

4. Camping trip

_____

5. Playing a game

_____

6. Building a house

_____

Problem Solving ▶ Reasoning

7. I am greater than the number of days in a week.
   I am less than the number of hours in a day.
   What number am I?   6   30   18   _____

 At Home Have your child explain to you which is longer, 10 days or 2 weeks. Repeat with similar examples.

Use a Table

MathTracks 2/19
Listen and Understand

Information you need to solve a problem can be in a table.

Use the clock and the table to help you solve the problem.

Every Monday, Lisa helps out at an animal shelter. How long does it take her to walk the dogs?

Helper's Activities

Activity	Start Time	End Time
Feed Cats	3:30	4:00
Walk Dogs	4:00	5:30
Sweep Floors	5:30	6:00

Start   End

4:00   5:30
_____   _____

Think
Use the start time and end time to find how long the activity lasts.

Dog walking lasts __1__ hour and __30__ minutes.

Use reasoning and the table to help you solve the problem.

Lisa leaves to go to the animal shelter at 3:00. She arrives on time. How long does it take her to get there?

Think
Use the time Lisa leaves and the time she arrives to find how long it takes her to get there.

What time does Lisa leave? _____:_____

What time does she begin her activities? _____:_____

How long does it take Lisa to get there? _____ minutes

Solve.

Use the table and a clock to help you.

Library Helpers		
Helper	Start Time	End Time
Dana	9:00	9:30
Philip	9:30	10:30
Marco	10:30	11:00
Elena	11:00	11:30

1. How long does Philip help out at the library?

   Think
   Philip starts at 9:30 and finishes at 10:30.

   Draw or write to explain.

   _____

2. Dana leaves for the library at **8:30**. She arrives on time. How long does it take her to get there?

   Think
   What time does Dana begin her help time?

   _____

Practice

3. Marco returns books to shelves during his help time. How long does Marco return books?

   _____

4. Elena gets home at **12:30**. How long does it take her to get home after she leaves the library?

   _____

452 four hundred fifty-two

Go on →

Name_____

Choose a Strategy

Solve.

1. There are 20 people who help clean up the gazebo. 15 more people come to help. How many people help in all?

Draw or write to explain.

_____ people

gazebo

2. There are 3 groups that clean up the garden. Each group has 5 children. How many children is that in all?

_____ children

garden

3. There are 10 people who help clean up the fountain. They start at 3:30 and finish one hour later. What time do they finish?

_____ : _____

fountain

4. **Multistep** The monument has 15 visitors every morning and 12 visitors every night. How many people visit the monument in two days?

_____ visitors

monument

At Home Have your child tell you what time you should leave if you have to be somewhere at 5:00 and it takes you 30 minutes to get there.

four hundred fifty-three **453**

Listen to your teacher read the problem.
Solve.

1. Wendy goes to soccer camp for 3 hours every Monday and Wednesday. How many hours does Wendy spend at soccer camp in 2 weeks?	Show your work using pictures, numbers, or words. _____ hours
2. Peter earns a quarter every time he walks his neighbor's dog. How much money does he earn if he walks the dog 3 times in one day?	 _____

Listen to your teacher read the problem.
Choose the correct answer.

3.   15 minutes   half hour   I hour $1\frac{1}{2}$ hours

        ○   ○   ○   ○

4.

        ○   ○   ○   ○

Name_____ **Quick Check**

Write the times.
Then write how much time has passed.

1.

_____ : _____ A.M.   _____ : _____ P.M.   _____ hours pass

Use the calendar to answer the question.

2. What is the date one week
   before September 26?

| September | | | | | | |
S	M	T	W	T	F	S
				1	2	3
4	5	6	7	8	9	10
11	12	13	14	15	16	17
18	19	20	21	22	23	24
25	26	27	28	29	30	

_____

3. Circle the longer amount
   of time.

   3 weeks   or   1 month

4. Circle the shorter amount
   of time.

   35 days   or   2 months

Solve.

5. How long does Tom's yard sale last?

_____

Saturday Yard Sales		
Sales	Start Time	End Time
Becky's	10:00	11:00
Tom's	2:30	3:00
Polly's	3:30	4:00

Mr. Thompson's class took a survey of their favorite books to read.

Favorite Books to Read

Book	Tally Marks
Animal Stories	卌 IIII
Adventure Stories	卌 卌 II
Fairy Tales	III
Sports	卌 I

Use the data in the chart to answer the questions.

1. How many children like Adventure Stories the best? _____

2. How many more children like Animal Stories than Fairy Tales? _____

3. Which type of book got the fewest votes? _____

4. Do more children like books about Sports or Animals? _____

5. How many children voted in the survey in all? _____

Math Challenge

Tweeters' Table

Use the clues to fill in the table with tally marks.

- 16 children in all voted for their favorite birds.

- There are 5 votes for parrots.

- There are 2 more votes for eagles than parrots.

- The same number of children voted for ducks and swans.

Bird	Tally
Parrots	
Ducks	
Swans	
Eagles	

Vocabulary (e • Glossary)

Draw a line to match.

1. **half-hour**   shows the days, weeks, and months in a year

2. **calendar**   30 minutes

3. **minute**   60 seconds

Concepts and Skills

Draw or write things you do that take the length of time.

4. About 5 seconds   5. About 10 minutes

Write the time.

6.    7.    8.    9.

_____ : _____   _____ : _____   _____ : _____   _____ : _____

Draw the minute hand to show the time.

10.    11.    12.    13.

10:45

9:10

1:35

8:00

Chapter Review/Test

Write the times.
Then write how much time has passed.

On Sale	Start Time	End Time	Sale Lasts
14.	____ : ____ P.M.	____ : ____ P.M.	____ hours
15. FRESH FRUIT	____ : ____ P.M.	____ : ____ P.M.	____ hours

Use the calendar to answer the question.

16. How many Mondays are in February? _____

17. What date in February is the second Friday? _____

FEBRUARY

S	M	T	W	T	F	S
			1	2	3	4	5
6	7	8	9	10	11	12
13	14	15	16	17	18	19
20	21	22	23	24	25	26
27	28					

Circle the longer amount of time.

18. 10 hours   or   1 day

19. 1 week   or   5 days

Problem Solving

Solve.
Use the table and a clock to help you.

20. How long does art last? _____

School Schedule	
Activity	**Time**
Gym	10:00 – 10:30
Art	10:30 – 11:00
Lunch	11:00 – 12:00

Name _____

Toys from Long Ago

WEEKLY **WR** READER®

Social Studies
Connection

English people came to live in North America long ago. They built and settled in towns like Williamsburg, VA. Today Williamsburg has houses and shops that show how the first settlers lived. One shop sells toys like the toys that children played with long ago.

1. Maria has **3** dimes and **5** nickels. How much more money does she need to buy this chalk?

59¢

Ciphering Chalk

ONE DOZEN WHITE CHALK STICKS

_____ ¢ more

2. Elias has these coins.

How much more money does he need to buy this slate?

85¢

_____ ¢ more

3. Marcel pays for these marbles with **3** quarters. How much change should he get?

66¢

_____ ¢

4. Tamika pays with a one-dollar bill for this whistle. She gets nickels for change. How many nickels does she get?

90¢

_____ nickels

This ball and stick game is called a bilbo catcher. Children toss the ball on the string and try to catch it in the cup.

1. Phi and Hana want to make a game like a bilbo catcher using a stick, a cup, and some string. They need 49¢ for string. Do they have enough money?

_____

2. Hana buys a ball for their game. It costs 55¢. Circle the coins she needs to pay the exact amount.

3. Yan buys a 70¢ cup for the game. She gives the clerk $1.00. She gets only dimes for change. How many dimes does she get?

4. The children see a bilbo catcher in a store. It costs 98¢. Draw coins to show that amount.

_____ dimes

Technology

Visit *Education Place* at **eduplace.com/kids/mw/** to learn more about this topic.

Vocabulary *e* • Glossary

Draw a line to match.

1. 60 minutes

2. 60 seconds

3. quarter

one minute

25¢

one hour

Concepts and Skills

Count on to find the value of the coins.

4.

_____ _____ _____ _____ □ ¢

Circle the value of the coins.

5.

less than $1.00   equal to $1.00

Add or subtract.
Write the ¢ in your answer.

6. 51¢
   + 19¢

7. 68¢
   − 29¢

8. 94¢
   − 7¢

9. 22¢
   + 18¢

Write the time.

10.

_____ : _____

11.

_____ : _____

Write each time.
Then, write how long the movie lasts.

12.

Movie	Start Time	End Time	How long does the movie last?
Super Dog	_____ : _____ P.M.	_____ : _____ P.M.	_____ hours

Use the calendar to answer the questions.

March

Sun.	Mon.	Tue.	Wed.	Thu.	Fri.	Sat.
		1	2	3	4	5
6	7	8	9	10	11	12
13	14	15	16	17	18	19
20	21	22	23	24	25	26
27	28	29	30	31		

13. What is the date of the third Tuesday?

_____

Problem Solving
Solve.
Use the table and a clock to help you.

Movie Schedule

Movie	Time
Super Dog	2:00 - 4:00
Banana Bunch	2:30 - 3:00
Dino-rama	3:00 - 4:00

14. How long does Banana Bunch last?

Draw or write to explain.

_____ minutes

15. Lance pays with a dollar bill for a cookie. He gets dimes for change. How many dimes does he get?

60¢

_____ dimes

462 four hundred sixty-two

Name ____________________

Performance Assessment

1. Show two ways to make 63¢.

Show your work with pictures, numbers, or words.

2. Luz buys a cap for 79¢. She gives the clerk $1.00. How much change does she get?

Show your work with pictures, numbers, or words.

_______ ¢

3. Mr. Ruiz goes to his shop at 9:00 in the morning. He closes for lunch at 12:00. How much time does he spend at work?

Show your work with pictures, numbers, or words.

_____ hours

4. At 1:00 Mr. Ruiz goes back to his shop and works until 5:30. How much time does Mr. Ruiz spend at work in the afternoon?

Show your work with pictures, numbers, or words.

_____

Travel Time

Use the picture and a clock to help
you answer the questions.

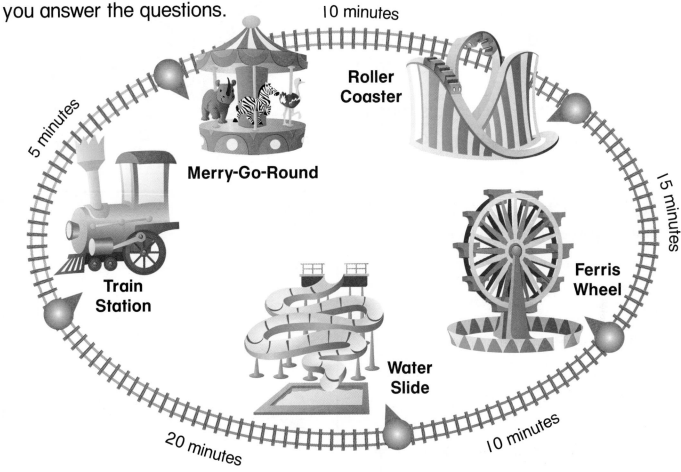

10 minutes

Roller
Coaster

5 minutes

Merry-Go-Round

15 minutes

Train
Station

Ferris
Wheel

Water
Slide

20 minutes

10 minutes

1. The train leaves the station at
1:00. It goes to the merry-go-
round. What time does it get
there?

_1_ : _05_

2. The train arrives at the water
slide at 1:40. What time does it
leave the Ferris wheel?

____ : ____

3. The train arrives at the Ferris
wheel at 1:30. What time did it
leave the roller coaster?

____ : ____

4. The train leaves the water slide
at 1:40. It goes to the train
station. What time does it get
there?

____ : ____

Technology

Visit *Education Place* at
eduplace.com/kids/mw/
for brain teasers.

Computer
Funny Money

Leonardo Leopard wants to buy a paintbrush for 79¢. What are two ways he can make 79¢?

Use the Coins and Bills models found at **eduplace.com/kids/mw/** to show equivalent amounts.

1. Click the **Change Mat** button. Choose **Two Numbers**. Click **Place Object**.

2. Click the **Quarter** 3 times.

3. Click the **Penny** 4 times.

4. Click [I 2 3] to check.

5. Click on the right side of the screen. Place another group of coins equal to 79¢.

Use the Coins and Bills models to show each amount two ways. Draw the coins.

	One Way	**Another Way**
I.  57¢		
2. 92¢		

Test-Taking Tips

· ·

When "N" is an answer choice, check all other choices carefully before choosing "N".

Be sure to mark the ○ of your answer neatly so that your choice is clear.

Multiple Choice

Fill in the ○ for the correct answer.

1. Mark the amount of money shown.

46¢	41¢	36¢	31¢
○	○	○	○

3. Lin buys a ball for 65¢. She pays with three quarters. What change does she get?

1¢	5¢	10¢	25¢
○	○	○	○

2. Choose a sign to make the sentence true.

71 ◯ 78

>	<	=	¢
○	○	○	○

4. What time does the clock show?

2:00	2:30	2:40	6:10
○	○	○	○

Multiple Choice

Fill in the ○ for the correct answer.
N means Not Here.

5. Find the sum.

$$\begin{array}{r} 60 \\ + \ 30 \\ \hline \end{array}$$

30	50	70	N
○	○	○	○

6. Mark the fraction of circles that are gray.

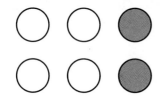

$\frac{2}{6}$	$\frac{1}{2}$	$\frac{2}{4}$	N
○	○	○	○

7. Mark how much time has passed.

1 hour	2 hours	3 hours	N
○	○	○	○

Open Response

Solve.

8. Draw a closed shape with three sides and three corners.

This shape is a _____ .

9. The clock shows 3:00. Explain how you can tell.

_____

_____

10. Write the total amount.

_____ ¢

Explain how you counted.

_____

_____

Test Prep on the Net
Visit *Education Place* at
eduplace.com/kids/mw/
for more test prep practice.

UNIT 7

Measurement

From the Read-Aloud Anthology

"The Whistling River"

from the book
Ol' Paul, The Mighty Logger

by Glen Rounds
illustrated by
Kevin Hawkes

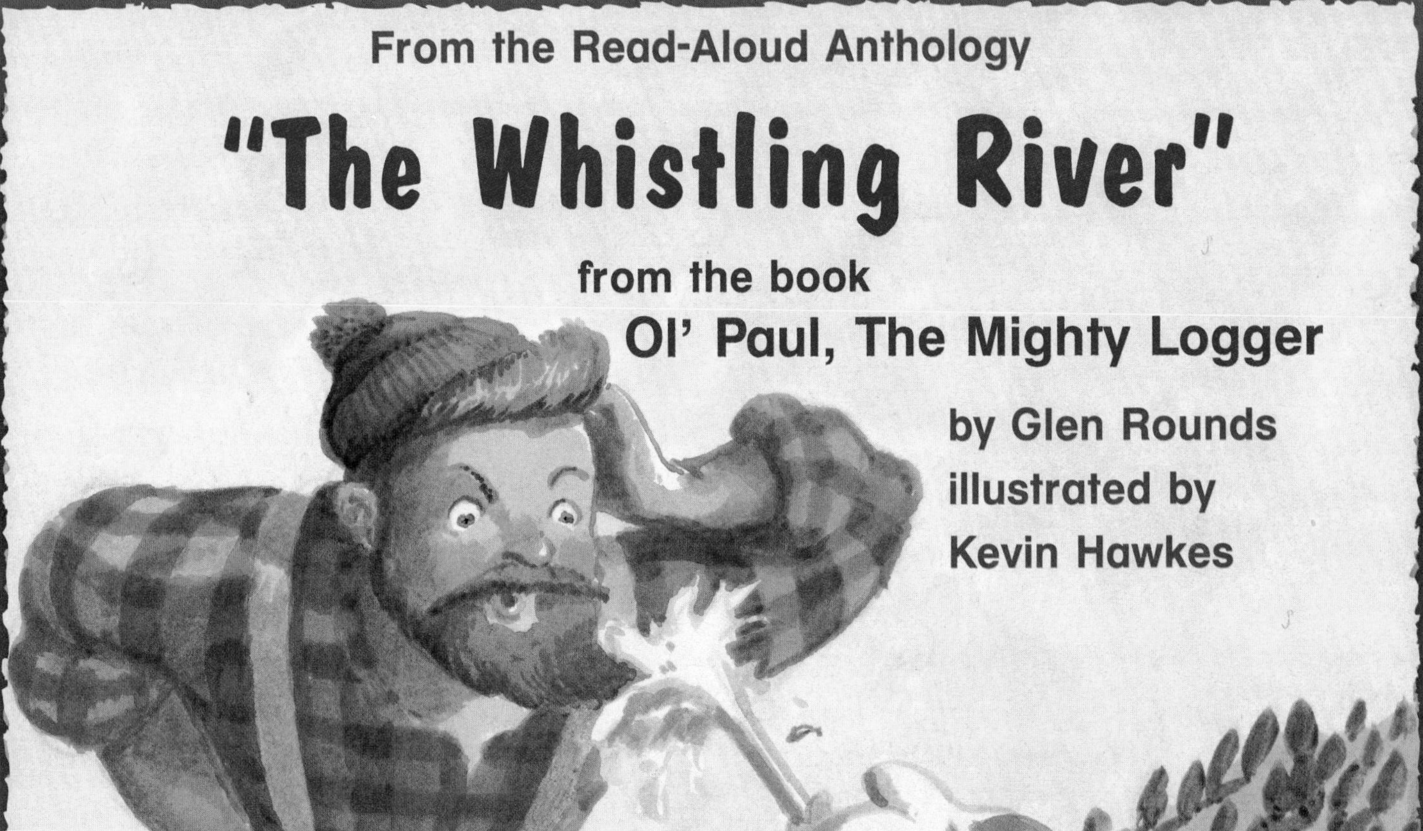

Access Prior Knowledge

This story will help you review

• Length, height, and weight
• Nonstandard units of length

469b from *The Whistling River*

It happened this way. It seems that Ol' Paul is sitting on a low hill one afternoon, combing his great curly beard with a pine tree, while he plans his winter operations. All of a sudden like, and without a word of warning, the river h'ists itself up on its hind legs and squirts about four thousands five hundred and nineteen gallons of river water straight in the center of Ol' Paul's whiskers.

Naturally Paul's considerably startled, but says nothing, figuring that if he pays it no mind, it'll go 'way and leave him be. But no sooner does he get settled back with his thinking and combing again, than the durn river squirts some more!

He decides that the only practical solution is to hitch Babe, the Mighty Blue Ox, to the river and let him yank it straight. Babe was so strong that he could pull mighty near anything that could be hitched to. His exact size, as I said before, is not known, for although it is said that he stood ninety-three hands high, it's not known whether that meant ordinary logger's hands, or hands the size of Paul's, which, of course, would be something else again.

Name_____

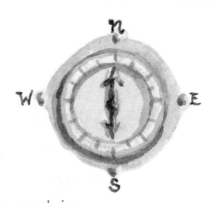

Use the story and pictures on pages 469b and 469c.
Find 2 objects to compare.

Draw or write to explain.

1. length

_____ is longer than _____.

2. weight

_____ is heavier than _____.

3. height

_____ is taller than _____.

The story says that Babe the Blue Ox "stood ninety-three hands high." That means someone measured the Ox's height using his or her hands.

Object	Estimate	Measure
4.		
5.		
6.		

Find 3 things in your classroom longer than your hand. Write the name of each object in the chart.
Estimate how many hands long or tall each object is.
Then measure.

7. Talk About It The story says that Paul wants to yank the river to make it straight. Will the length of the river be the same? Why or why not?

MATH at Home

Dear Family,

My class is starting Unit 7. I will be learning about measurement. These pages show some of what I will learn and have activities for us to do together.

From, _____

Vocabulary

These are some words I will use in this unit.

inch (in.) **foot, feet (ft)**	Customary units used to measure length	**centimeter (cm)** **meter (m)**	Metric units used to measure length
	12 inches = 1 foot		100 centimeters = 1 meter
gallon (gal)	A customary unit used to measure how much something holds	**liter** **milliliters (ML)**	Metric units used to measure how much something holds
pound (lb)	A customary unit used to measure weight	**kilogram (kg)**	A metric unit used to measure how heavy an object is
degrees Fahrenheit (°F)	The customary unit used to measure temperature	**degrees Celsius (°C)**	The metric unit used to measure temperature
perimeter	The distance around a plane shape	**area**	The number of square units in a region

Some other words I will use are **yard, cup, pint, quart, ounce, temperature,** and **thermometer**.

Turn the page for more.

Vocabulary Activity

Let's work together to complete these sentences.

1. Fahrenheit and Celsius are units that measure _____.

2. The distance around a plane shape is the _____.

How To measure to the nearest inch

In this unit, I will learn how to measure length using standard units. This is an example of how I will learn to measure length using an inch ruler.

How to use an inch ruler.

Measure.

Be sure to place the rule correctly.

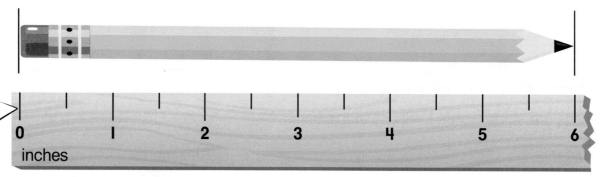

Line up the object with this mark.

The pencil is about ___6___ inches long.

Literature

These books link to the math in this unit. We can look for them at the library.

Room for Ripley
by Stuart J. Murphy
Illustrated by Sylvie Wickstrom
(Harper Collins, 1999)

Counting on Frank
Written by Rod Clement

Let's read together!

Technology

We can visit *Education Place* at **eduplace.com/parents/mw/** for the Math Lingo game, *e* Glossary, and more games and activities to do together.

Length

CHAPTER 17

INVESTIGATION

What are the different ways to talk about the size of a book?

Five is Fine

Find five things that are about five cubes long.
Draw them here.

Nonstandard Units

MathTracks 2/20
Listen and Understand

Estimate the **length** and measure with paper clips.

Objective
Estimate and measure length using nonstandard units.

Vocabulary
length

Line up the units with the end of the object.

Estimate: about ____4____ paper clips long

Measure: about ____4____

You can use different units to measure the same object. Estimate and measure with cubes.

Estimate before you measure.

Estimate: about ____6____ cubes long

Measure: about ____6____

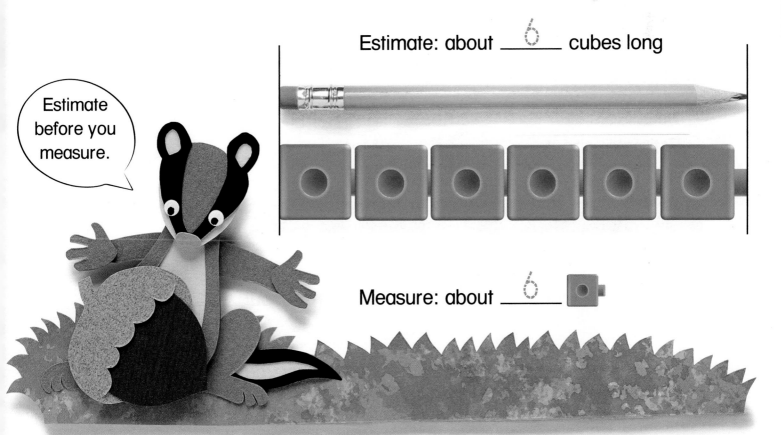

Guided Practice

Think
I need to line up the units with the end of the yarn.

Use  and ⬛.

Estimate the length with the unit shown.
Then measure.

1.

Estimate: about _____ ⬭   Measure: about _____ ⬭

2.

Estimate: about _____ ⬭   Measure: about _____ ⬭

3.

Estimate: about _____ ⬛   Measure: about _____ ⬛

4.

Estimate: about _____ ⬛   Measure: about _____ ⬛

5.

Estimate: about _____ ⬛   Measure: about _____ ⬛

TEST TIPS **Explain Your Thinking** Which is the longest yarn? Would it take more cubes or paper clips to match the length?

476 four hundred seventy-six

Go on ➡

Name _____

Practice

Find the real object.

Use ⬭ and ◨.

Estimate the length with each unit.
Then measure.

> Remember to line up the units with the end of the object.

Object	Estimate	Measure
1. MY MATH	 about  _____ ⬭ about  _____ ◨	about  _____ ⬭ about  _____ ◨
2.	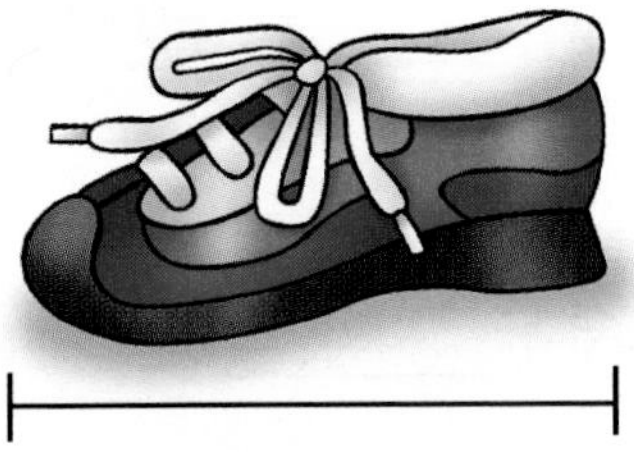 about  _____ ⬭ about  _____ ◨	about  _____ ⬭ about  _____ ◨
3.	 about  _____ ⬭ about  _____ ◨	about  _____ ⬭ about  _____ ◨
4.	 about  _____ ⬭ about  _____ ◨	about  _____ ⬭ about  _____ ◨
5.	 about  _____ ⬭ about  _____ ◨	about  _____ ⬭ about  _____ ◨

Problem Solving ▶ Measurement Sense

Use larger units to measure larger things.

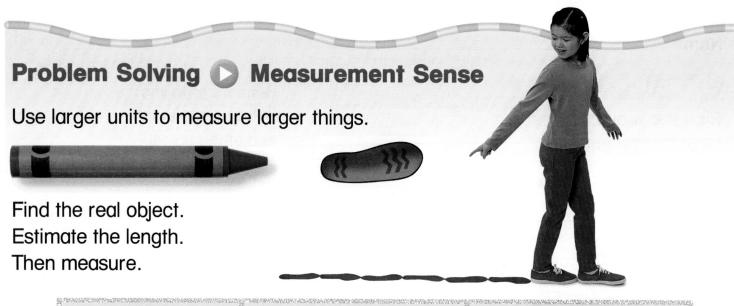

Find the real object.
Estimate the length.
Then measure.

Object	Estimate	Measure
1. 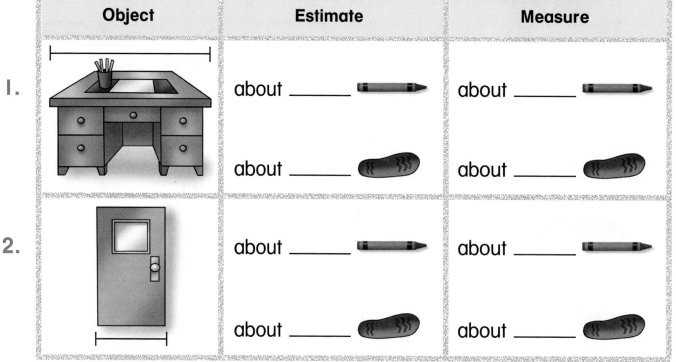	about _____ 🖍 about _____ 👟	about _____ 🖍 about _____ 👟
2.	about _____ 🖍 about _____ 👟	about _____ 🖍 about _____ 👟

3. Lily wants to measure the length of her classroom.
   Circle the best unit to use. Explain why.

_____

_____

4. **Write About It** Why is it important for people to use the same units to

   describe length? _____

   _____

   _____

At Home Have your child measure the length of a room by stepping heel to toe and counting the steps. You do the same and discuss the results.

Name_____

Activity: Inches

You can estimate and measure length using **inches.** Length can tell how tall, how long, or how wide.

Objective
Estimate and measure length to the nearest inch.
Vocabulary
inch   inches
inch ruler

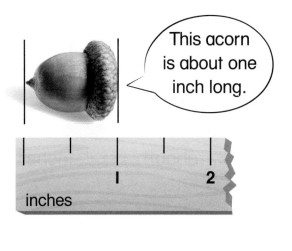

This acorn is about one inch long.

inches

Work Together

Work with a partner to estimate and measure.
Use an **inch ruler.**

First estimate.
About how long is the crayon?

An inch is this long.

1 inch

The crayon is about ___3___ inches long.

Then measure.
Be sure to place the ruler correctly.

Line up the object with this mark.

The crayon is about ___3___ inches long.

inches

On Your Own

Find the real object. Estimate the length.
Then use a ruler to measure to the nearest inch.

Object	Estimate	Measure
1.	about _____ inches	about _____ inches
2. ERASER	about _____ inches	about _____ inches
3. Glue	about _____ inches	about _____ inches
4.	about _____ inches	about _____ inches

5. Write the four lengths above in order from shortest to longest.

_____ inches   _____ inches   _____ inches   _____ inches

Compare the real objects. Circle the longer one.

6.

7.

Go on

Name_____

Choose three more objects to measure.
Draw them in the chart.
Estimate. Then measure.

	Object	Estimate	Measure
1.	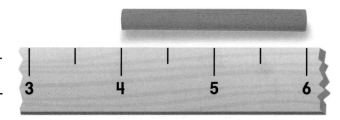	about _____ inches	about _____ inches
2.		about _____ inches	about _____ inches
3.		about _____ inches	about _____ inches
4.		about _____ inches	about _____ inches

5. **Write About It** Lee says his chalk is about 2 inches long. Is he correct? How do you know?_____

_____

_____

6. **Talk About It** How can you measure something that is longer than your ruler?

At Home Have your child estimate the length of three items in your home, then measure each item with a ruler. Compare the measures to the estimates.

Now Try This **Measure to the Nearest Half Inch**

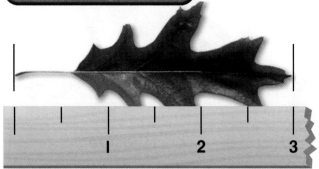

This leaf is about 3 inches long.

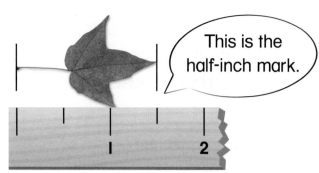

This is the half-inch mark.

This leaf is about $1\frac{1}{2}$ inches long.

Circle the best measure.

Think
Does the feather line up closer to an inch mark or a $\frac{1}{2}$ inch mark?

1.

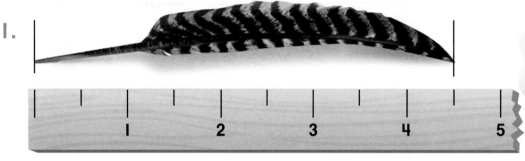

about 5 inches   about $4\frac{1}{2}$ inches   about 4 inches

2.

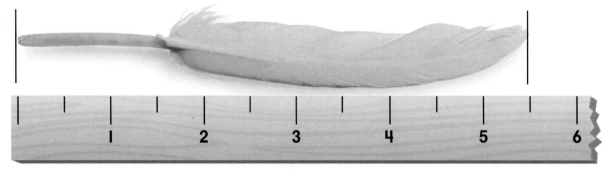

about 6 inches   about 5 inches   about $5\frac{1}{2}$ inches

3.

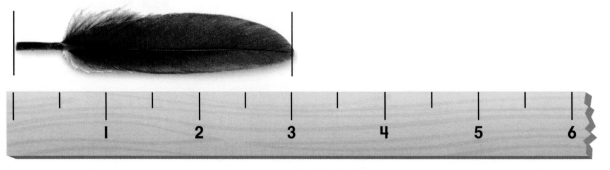

about 3 inches   about $3\frac{1}{2}$ inches   about $4\frac{1}{2}$ inches

Name_____

Activity: Inches and Feet

MathTracks 2/21
Listen and Understand

An **inch** ruler can be used to measure in inches and **feet.**

Objective
Estimate and measure to the nearest inch or foot.

Vocabulary
inch (in.)
foot, feet (ft)

My folk tale journal is about 12 inches long.

This is an easy way to write inches.

12 **in.** = 1 **foot**

My desk is about 2 feet tall.

This is an easy way to write foot or feet.

_____ **ft**

Work Together

Find the real object.
Estimate. Then measure in the unit shown.

	Object	Estimate	Measure
1.	2+4=	about _____ ft	about _____ ft
2.	(crayon box)	about _____ in.	about _____ in.
3.	(chair)	about _____ in.	about _____ in.

TEST TIPS **Explain Your Thinking** When might you measure in inches instead of feet?

On Your Own

Find the real object.
Use inches or feet.
Estimate then measure.

Reminder
Remember to write **in.** or **ft** to label your answer.

Object	Estimate	Measure
1.	about _____ ft_____	about _____ _____
2.	about _____ _____	about _____ _____
3.	about _____ _____	about _____ _____

4. Write the three lengths above in order from shortest to longest.

_____   _____   _____

Draw an object to measure.
Use inches or feet. Estimate then measure.

Draw the object	Estimate	Measure
5.	about _____ _____	about _____ _____

6. Talk About It The boys need a string that is more than 1 foot long. Marco's string is 13 inches long. Is it long enough? How do you know?

484 four hundred eighty-four

At Home Have your child choose an object to measure in inches and an object to measure in feet.

Name _____

Foot and Yard

MathTracks 2/22
Listen and Understand

The **distance** from a door knob to the floor is about 3 feet.

3 feet = 1 **yard**

A **yardstick** is 3 feet.

This distance is about 2 yards.

This distance is about 6 feet.

Objective
Estimate and measure to the nearest foot or yard.

Vocabulary
distance
yard
yardstick

Guided Practice

Use feet or yards to estimate.
Then measure.

Find	Estimate	Measure
1. How far apart?	about ____ yards _____	about ____ _____
2. How tall? 2+4=	about ____ _____	about ____ _____

3. List objects in your classroom for each length shown in the chart.

Shorter than 1 yard	About 1 yard	Longer than 1 yard

TEST TIPS **Explain Your Thinking** Is a distance of 4 feet greater or less than 1 yard? How can you tell without measuring?

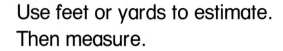

Remember to write the unit you use.

Use feet or yards to estimate.
Then measure.

Find	Estimate	Measure
1. How tall?	about ____ _____	about ____ _____
2. How wide?	about ____ _____	about ____ _____
3. How long?	about ____ _____	about ____ _____
4. How far apart?	about ____ _____	about ____ _____

Problem Solving ▶ Measurement Sense

Circle the better estimate.

Draw or write to explain.

5. Lionel and Sara see an owl in a tree. About how tall is the tree?

    4 inches   4 yards

 At Home Help your child name objects in your home that are shorter than, longer than, or about the same as 1 yard. Use a yardstick or ruler to check.

Measurement Hunt

Players: teams of 2, 3, or 4

What You Need: an inch ruler and a yardstick

How to Play

1. Work in a team.

2. Find objects that you think measure 3 inches, 8 inches, 1 foot, 2 feet, and 1 yard. Measure the objects.

3. Draw or write the name for each object.

4. The first team to find all 5 objects wins.

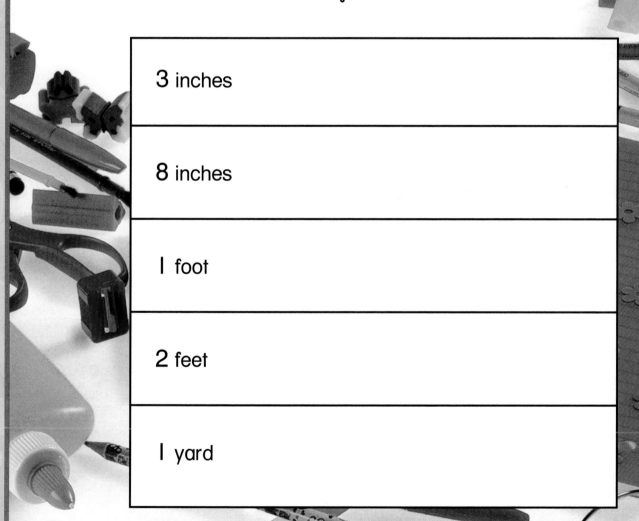

3 inches
8 inches
1 foot
2 feet
1 yard

Quick Check

Use the unit shown.
Estimate the length. Then measure.

1.

Estimate: about _____   Measure: about _____

Estimate: about _____   Measure: about _____

Estimate the length.
Then use a ruler to measure to the nearest inch.

2.

Estimate: about _____ inches   Measure: about _____ inches

3.

Estimate: about _____ inches   Measure: about _____ inches

Complete the sentence.
Write **more than** or **less than**.

4. 14 inches is _____ 1 foot.

5. 8 inches is _____ 1 foot.

6. Write these lengths in order from shortest to longest.

| 1 yard | 2 feet | 13 inches |

_____   _____   _____

Name_____

Centimeters and Meters

Objective
Estimate and measure in centimeters and meters.

Vocabulary
centimeter (cm)
meter (m)
meter stick

Centimeter and **meter** are two more units you can use to estimate and measure length.

This button is about
1 **centimeter** wide.

about _____ **cm**

Use a centimeter ruler to measure short lengths.

A door is about
1 **meter** wide.

about _____ **m**

Use a **meter stick** to measure long lengths.

A meter is 100 cm.

Guided Practice

Find the real object.
Use centimeters or meters.
Estimate then measure.

Think
My finger is about 1 centimeter wide. I can use it to estimate.

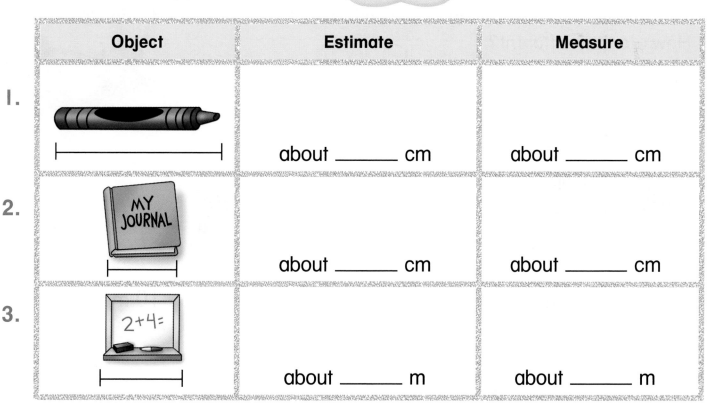

Object	Estimate	Measure
1.	about _____ cm	about _____ cm
2.	about _____ cm	about _____ cm
3.	about _____ m	about _____ m

TEST TIPS **Explain Your Thinking** Look at the objects you measured. Which is the longest? Which is the shortest? How do you know?

Remember to label your answer with cm or m.

Find the real object.
Use centimeters or meters.
Estimate then measure.

Object	Estimate	Measure
1.	about _____ __m__	about _____ _____
2.	about _____ _____	about _____ _____
3.	about _____ _____	about _____ _____

4. Order the lengths from shortest to longest.

| 1 m | 1 cm | 1 in. | 1 ft |

_____   _____   _____   _____

5. **Talk About It** How are the units centimeter, meter, foot, and inch alike? How are they different?

Problem Solving ▶ Measurement Sense

About how long or tall is the real object?
Circle the better estimate.

6.

   15 cm long   50 cm long

7.

   1 m tall   10 m tall

8.

   3 cm long   3 m long

9.

   10 m tall   10 cm tall

 At Home Ask your child to name objects he or she would measure in centimeters and objects he or she would measure in meters.

Name _____

Perimeter

 **MathTracks 2**/23
Listen and Understand

The distance around a plane shape is its **perimeter.**

Find the perimeter of the classroom floor.

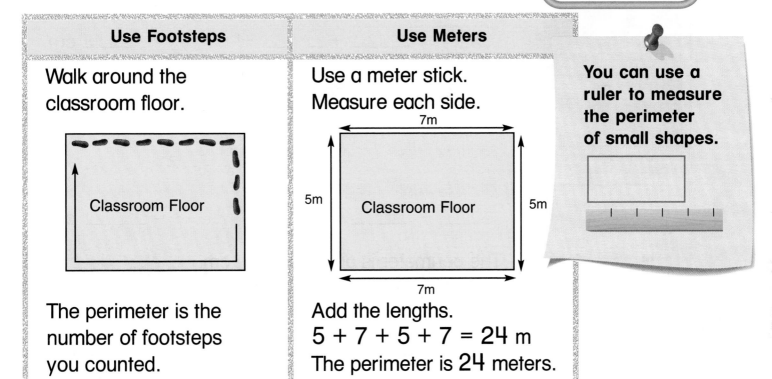

Use Footsteps	**Use Meters**
Walk around the classroom floor.	Use a meter stick. Measure each side.
Classroom Floor	Classroom Floor
The perimeter is the number of footsteps you counted.	Add the lengths. 5 + 7 + 5 + 7 = 24 m The perimeter is 24 meters.

You can use a ruler to measure the perimeter of small shapes.

Guided Practice

Think
I need to measure each side to the nearest centimeter.

Use a centimeter ruler.
Measure and write the length of each side.
Add to find the perimeter.

1.  _____ + _____ + _____ + _____ = _____ cm

   The perimeter is about _____ cm.

2.  _____ + _____ + _____ + _____ = _____ cm

   The perimeter is about _____ cm.

TEST TIPS **Explain Your Thinking** How many sides do you need to measure to find the perimeter of a square? Tell why.

Measure each side to the nearest centimeter.

Use a centimeter ruler.
Measure and write the length of each side.
Add to find the perimeter.

1.

4 cm + _____ + _____ + _____ = _____ cm

The perimeter is about _____ cm.

2.

_____ + _____ + _____ + _____ = _____ cm

The perimeter is about _____ cm.

3.

_____ + _____ + _____ + _____ = _____ cm

The perimeter is about _____ cm.

Problem Solving ▶ Reasoning

4. Mai wants to put a fence around her garden. How much fencing does she need?

   about _____ m

6 m

3 m

5. **Talk About It** Explain how you found the perimeter of Mai's garden.

At Home Help your child find the perimeter of objects in your home such as table tops and book covers.

Name_____

Activity: Area

MathTracks 2/24
Listen and Understand

You can find the **area** of a plane shape by using **square units.**

square unit

Work Together

1. Cover the shape with square units. Count how many square units.

The area is about ___3___ square units.

2. You can estimate the area of a plane shape.

Use what you know about the size of a square unit to estimate the area.

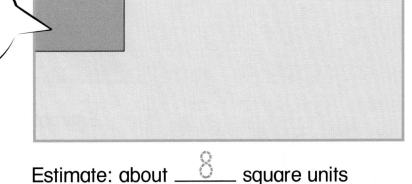

Estimate: about ___8___ square units

3. Use the square unit.

Estimate the area.
Then find the area.

Estimate: about _____ square units

Measure: about _____ square units

Use square units.

Estimate.
Then find the area of the shape.

1.

Think
I can put 1 square unit in the corner of the shape to help me estimate.

Estimate: about _____ square units

Measure: about _____ square units

2.

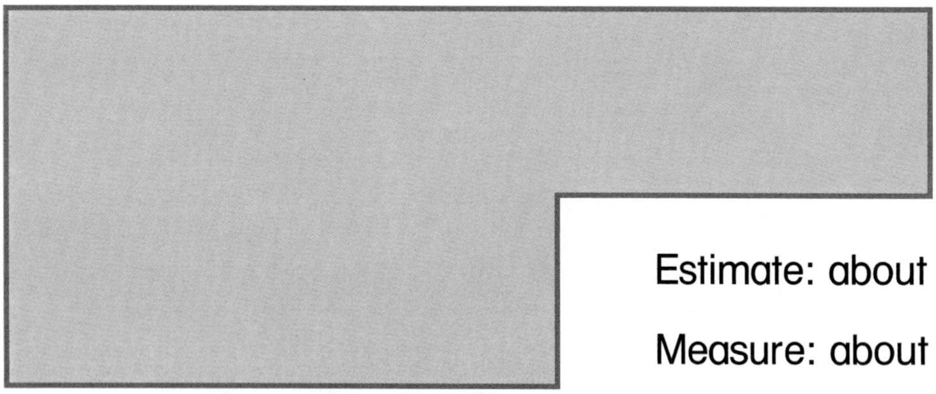

Estimate: about _____ square units

Measure: about _____ square units

3.

Estimate: about _____ square units

Measure: about _____ square units

Go on

Name_____

Sometimes you can find the area of a shape using grid paper.
Look at the shape on the grid paper.
Find the area.

1.

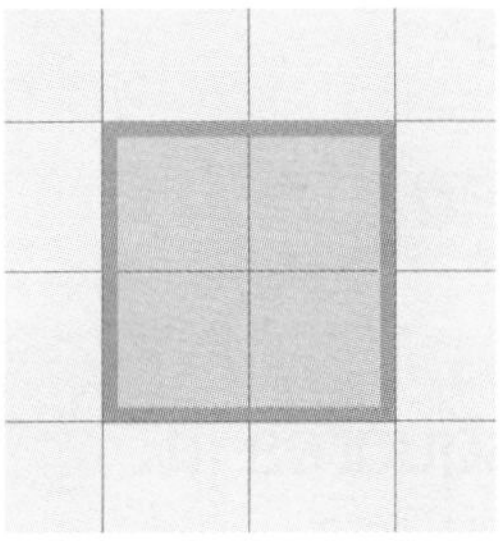

_____4_____ square units

2.

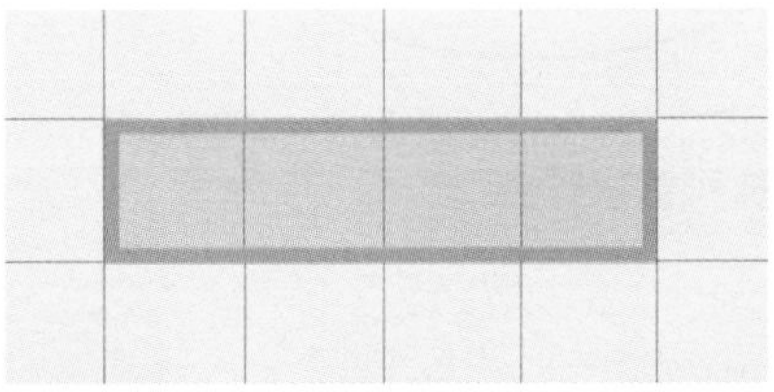

_____ square units

3.

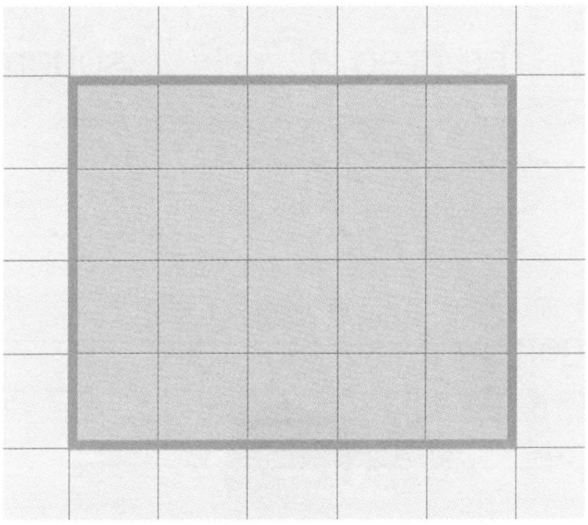

_____ square units

4.

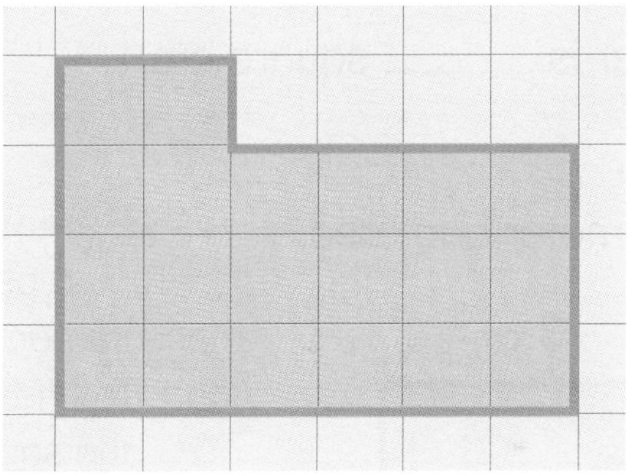

_____ square units

5.

_____ square units

6. **Write About It** If two shapes have
the same area, are they always the
same shape? Draw a picture to show
how you know.

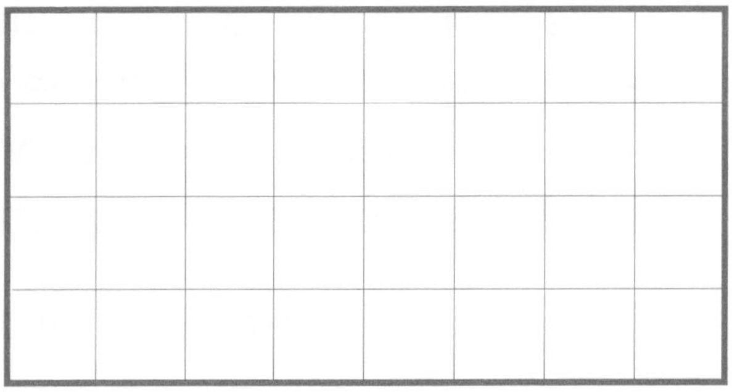

At Home Ask your child to tell you how he or she found the
area for one of the rectangles in this lesson.

Find the perimeter and area of this shape.

This side is 1 centimeter long.

This is 1 square centimeter.

Perimeter	**Area**

Find the length of each side of the red shape. Then add.

__1__ + __3__ + __1__ + __3__ = __8__ cm

The perimeter is __8__ square cm.

Count the squares in the red shape.

There are __3__ squares.

The area is __3__ square cm.

Find the perimeter and area.

Remember
To find perimeter measure each side, then add. To find area count the squares.

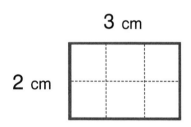

3 cm

2 cm

1. The perimeter is _____ cm.

   The area is _____ square cm.

2. **Talk About It** Explain how you found the answers for Exercise 1.

3. Jonah makes a patch to cover a hole in his shirt. The area of the patch is 4 square centimeters. The perimeter is 10 centimeters. Circle which shows the shape and size of his patch.

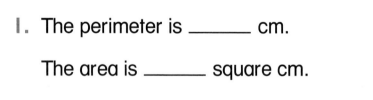

4. **Talk About It** Explain how you found the answer for Exercise 3.

Name_____

Use a Picture

Objective
Use a picture to solve problems.

You can use a picture to solve a problem.

Use a ruler to measure.
Tonia wants to make this bookmark.

How long a piece of ribbon does she need?

Measure the bookmark.

The bookmark is ___13___ cm long.

Tonia's ribbon should be ___13___ cm long.

Think
I line up the centimeter ruler correctly to measure.

Use the measurements in the picture.
Chris wants to put another piece of yarn around the picture. How much yarn does she need?

Think
I do not have to measure. The lengths of the sides are shown in the picture.

10 cm

8 cm   **8 cm**

10 cm

You need to find the perimeter.
Add the measures.

___10___ + ___8___ + ___10___ + ___8___ = ___36___ cm

Chris needs ___36___ cm of yarn.

Use the picture to solve the problem.

1. Stuart measures the top of this box in square tiles. What is the area?

Draw or write to explain.

> **Think**
> I can count the squares to find the area.

_____ square tiles

2. Christina needs a hair clip that is about 5 cm long. Should she buy the pink clip or the blue clip?

> **Think**
> I need to measure in centimeters.

_____ clip

3. Berit wants to make a bracelet just like this one. How long will her bracelet be?

_____ centimeters

4. Travis makes a fence to go around his garden. How much fencing does he use?

6 meters

5 meters 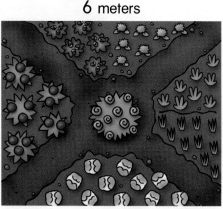 5 meters

6 meters

_____ meters

Go on

Name_____

Choose a Strategy

Solve.

1. Yasmin makes a pattern. She uses squirrel footprints and acorns. Draw what comes next in the pattern.

Draw or write to explain.

squirrel

2. Aldo buys 84 flowers to make a wreath. Which two bags of flowers does he buy?

24 36 48

wreath

bag of _____ and bag of _____

3. Donna buys two bags of rocks for her aquarium. The bags cost 39¢ and 25¢. How much does Donna pay for the rocks?

aquarium

_____ ¢

4. **Multistep** Kevin uses 4 pieces of yarn to finish his nature collage. Each piece is this long.

How many centimeters does Kevin need?

collage

_____ cm

 At Home Ask your child to create a problem similar to Exercise 4 using a picture or item from home, then solve the problem.

Listen to your teacher read the problem.
Solve.

1. Mr. Portela put this rug in his office.
The rug is the exact size of the room.
What is the perimeter of
Mr. Portela's office?

5 meters

3 meters   3 meters

5 meters

Show your work using pictures,
numbers, or words.

_____ meters

2. What is the area of the rug in
Mr. Portela's office?

_____ square meters

Listen to your teacher read the problem.
Choose the correct answer.

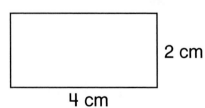

2 cm

4 cm

3. 6 centimeters   10 centimeters   12 centimeters   16 centimeters
    ○   ○   ○   ○

4.   1 yard   14 inches   2 feet   8 inches
    ○   ○   ○   ○

Name_____

About how long or tall is the real object?
Circle the better estimate.

1.

4 cm long   15 cm long

2.

1 m tall   10 m tall

3. Use a centimeter ruler.
   Measure and record the length of each side.
   Add to find the perimeter.

   _____ + _____ + _____ + _____ = _____

   The perimeter is _____ cm.

4. This is one square unit ☐.
   Estimate.
   Then find the area of the shape.

   Estimate: about _____ square units

   Measure: about _____ square units

Use the picture to solve the problem.

5. Jeremy wants to make a bookmark the same length as this one.
   How many centimeters long should the piece of paper be?

   _____ cm

Add.

1. 7 +50	2. 24 + 7	3. 6 +64	4. 77 + 2	5. 85 + 9
6. 15 +19	7. 28 +35	8. 73 +20	9. 56 +18	10. 25 +25
11. 31 +26	12. 34 +14	13. 23 +76	14. 44 +19	15. 21 +49

Rewrite the addends. Add.

16. 71 + 26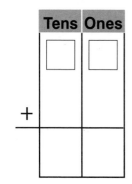

17. 63 + 3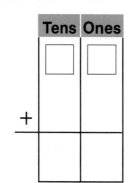

18. 27 + 55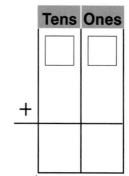

19. 8 + 14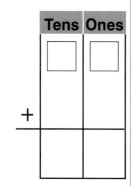

Science Connection

Pine Cones

Pine cones are found all over the
United States. They come from pine trees.
There are many different types of pine cones.

Cara finds a pine cone that is 14 inches long.
Is the pine cone longer or shorter than 1 foot? _____

Name_____

Vocabulary   *e* • Glossary

Use the word in a sentence.

1. **inch** _____

_____

2. **centimeter** _____

_____

Concepts and Skills

Estimate the length.
Then use a ruler to measure to the nearest inch.

3.

Estimate: about _____ inches   **Measure:** about _____ inches

Circle the best measure.

4.

about 5 inches   about 6 inches   about $5\frac{1}{2}$ inches

Complete the sentence.
Write **more than** or **less than**.

5. 11 inches is _____ 1 foot.   6. 4 feet is _____ 1 yard.

About how long or tall is the real object?
Circle the better estimate.

7.

14 centimeters   4 meters

8.

7 centimeters   1 meter

Use a centimeter ruler.
Measure and record the length of each side.
Add to find the perimeter.

9.

_____ + _____ + _____ + _____ = _____ cm

Problem Solving

Use the picture to solve the problem.

10. Sasha wants to make a tile
design. How many tiles will she
use to cover the shape?

Draw or write to explain.

1 tile   Sasha's Design

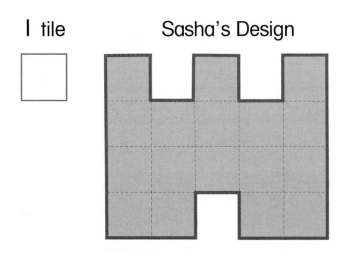

_____ tiles

Weight, Capacity, and Temperature

CHAPTER 18

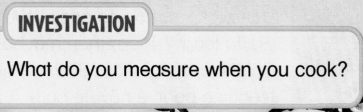

INVESTIGATION

What do you measure when you cook?

People Using Math

Julia Child

Do you know how to cook? Would you like to learn? If so, then maybe Julia Child can teach you. She has been teaching people how to cook for nearly 40 years.

Julia's favorite kind of food to cook is French food, and her favorite ingredient is butter. She can also cook many other kinds of food — even macaroni and cheese. People have been able to watch Julia cook on her television shows. They can find her recipes in cookbooks.

Match the picture with a tool Julia would use to measure the item.

1.    

2. 

3. 

Name_____

Activity: Cups, Pints, Quarts, and Gallons

 **MathTracks 2**/25
Listen and Understand

Use units such as **cups**, **pints**, **quarts**, and **gallons**
to measure how much a container can hold.

Objective
Use cups, pints,
quarts, and gallons
to estimate and
measure capacity.

Vocabulary
cup (c)
pint (pt)
quart (qt)
gallon (gal)

 Work Together

Find how many cups are in a quart.

 Step 1

Estimate.
Write your estimate in the table below.

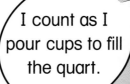 **Step 2**

Measure.
Write the number of cups
it takes to fill the quart.

Complete the table.

About how
many cups of water
will a quart hold?

I count as I
pour cups to fill
the quart.

	How many?	Estimate	Measure
1.	cups in a quart	_____ cups	_____ cups
2.	cups in a pint	_____ cups	_____ cups
3.	pints in a quart	_____ pints	_____ pints
4.	pints in a gallon	_____ pints	_____ pints
5.	quarts in a gallon	_____ quarts	_____ quarts

2 cups = 1 pint
2 pints = 1 quart
4 quarts = 1 gallon

Use cup, pint, quart, and gallon containers.
Find out which amount is greater. Circle it.
Circle both if they are the same.

1. 2 quarts   1 gallon

2. 4 pints   2 quarts

3. 3 cups   1 pint

4. 3 pints   1 quart

5. 3 quarts   1 gallon

6. 9 pints   1 gallon

Write the number that makes each sentence true.

7. 4 cups = _____ pints

8. 4 pints = _____ cups

9. _____ quarts = 12 cups

10. 2 gallons = _____ quarts

11. 2 quarts = _____ pints

12. _____ cups = 2 pints

Go on

Name_____

On Your Own

Find the container and the measuring tool.
Estimate. Then measure to the nearest unit.

	Container	Estimate	Measure
1.	mug	about _____ cups	about _____ cups
2.	paper cup	about _____ cups	about _____ cups
3.	pitcher	about _____ pints	about _____ pints
4.	bucket	about _____ quarts	about _____ quarts

Use the information in the table.

5. Which holds more? Circle it.

   mug   paper cup

6. Which holds less? Circle it.

   pitcher   bucket

7. Which container holds the most?

   _____

8. List the containers in order from
   the one that holds the least to
   the one that holds the most.

   _____ _____ _____ _____

It takes almost
5 cups to fill this vase.
The vase holds about
5 cups.

9. **Talk About It** Which unit would be best to use to find out how
   much water a bathtub can hold? Why?

At Home Using a cup measure, have your child estimate and
then measure about how many cups different containers hold.

Now Try This Ounces

An **ounce** is another unit you can use to measure how much a container will hold.

A large spoon can hold about 1 ounce.
An ounce is much less than a cup.

8 ounces = 1 cup

1 ounce   8 ounces   1 cup

Does the item hold more or less than 1 ounce?
Circle the answer.

1.

   more   less

2.

   more   less

3.

   more   less

Write >, <, or =.

4. 1 cup $\bigcirc$ 8 ounces

5. 2 cups $\bigcirc$ 10 ounces

6. 18 ounces $\bigcirc$ 2 cups

7. 14 ounces $\bigcirc$ 1 cup

8. 16 ounces $\bigcirc$ 2 cups

9. 20 ounces $\bigcirc$ 3 cups

10. **Talk About It** Would it be better to use ounces or cups to measure how much water a fishbowl can hold? Is there a better unit to use? Why?

Name_____

Activity: Liters

MathTracks 2/26
Listen and Understand

You can use units such as **liters** and **milliliters** to measure how much a container can hold.

Objective
Use liters to estimate and measure capacity; understand milliliters.
Vocabulary
liter (L)   milliliter (mL)

This holds about 1 milliliter. A milliliter is much less than a liter.

less than 1 liter   **1 liter**   **more than 1 liter**

Work Together

Work with a partner.
Use a liter measure.

Will this pitcher hold more than, less than, or about the same amount as the liter?

If I can empty the whole liter into the pitcher then I know the pitcher holds a liter or more.

Step 1

Estimate. Write **more than**, **less than**, or **about** in the table.

Step 2

Measure. Write **more than**, **less than**, or **about** in the table.

Complete the table.

	Container	Estimate	Measure
1.	pitcher	_____ 1 liter	_____ 1 liter
2.	drinking glass	_____ 1 liter	_____ 1 liter
3.	bucket	_____ 1 liter	_____ 1 liter

The fish bowl holds at least 1 liter. How many more liters will it hold?

I count as I pour each liter into the bowl. The bowl holds about 7 liters.

Work Together

Find the container.
Estimate how many liters it holds.
Measure.

	Container	Estimate	Measure
1.	juice bottle	about _____ liters	about _____ liters
2.	tea pot	about _____ liters	about _____ liters
3.	vase	about _____ liters	about _____ liters
4.	bowl	about _____ liters	about _____ liters

On Your Own

Circle the better estimate.

5.

It takes about 10 drops to make a milliliter.

100 milliliters   100 liters

6.

4 milliliters   4 liters

7. **Talk About It** Would a fish tank hold about 2 liters or about 20 liters? Explain your answer.

 At Home Have your child use a liter measure to find if kitchen containers hold more than, less than, or about 1 liter of water.

Name_____

Activity: Pounds and Ounces

You can measure **weight** in **pounds** and **ounces** .

16 ounces = 1 pound

A slice of bread weighs 1 ounce.

The pasta weighs 1 pound.

Objective
Use pounds and ounces to estimate and measure weight.

Vocabulary
weight   pound (lb)
ounce (oz)

1 ounce   **1 pound**

Work Together

Work with a partner.

Use a balance scale, a 1-pound measure, and a 1-ounce measure.

Step 1

Estimate. Then write **more than**, **less than**, or **about** in the table.

Does the eraser weigh more than, less than, or about the same as 1 pound?

Step 2

Measure. Then write **more than**, **less than**, or **about** in the table.

The eraser is up. It is less than 1 pound.

Complete the table. Write **more than**, **less than** or **about**.

	Object	Estimate	Measure
1.	stapler	_____ 1 ounce	_____ 1 ounce
2.	math book	_____ 1 pound	_____ 1 pound
3.	a shoe	_____ 1 pound	_____ 1 pound

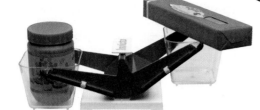

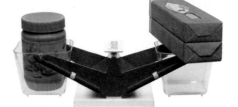

A box of pasta weighs 1 pound.

more than 1 pound   **about 2 pounds**

Find objects that weigh more than 1 pound.
Write their names in the table.

Hold an object in one hand.
Hold 1-pound measures in the other hand.

Estimate the weight.

Then use a balance scale and 1-pound measures to check.

	Object Name	Estimate	Measure
1.	_____	about _____ pounds	about _____ pounds
2.	_____	about _____ pounds	about _____ pounds
3.	_____	about _____ pounds	about _____ pounds
4.	_____	about _____ pounds	about _____ pounds

5. Write the four weights in order from lightest to heaviest.

_____ pounds   _____ pounds   _____ pounds   _____ pounds

6. **Talk About It** Which weighs more, a pound of feathers or 16 ounces of rocks? Explain why.

At Home Find 3 similar size items. Have your child put them in order according to their weights.

Name_____

Activity: Kilograms and Grams

You can use **kilograms** and **grams** to measure how heavy an object is.

Objective
Use kilograms and grams to estimate and measure mass.

Vocabulary
kilogram (kg)
gram (g)

> The grape is about 1 gram.

> The can of tomatoes is about 1 kilogram.

I kg = 1000g

1 kilogram

Work Together

Work in groups. Use a balance scale and a 1-kilogram weight.

Step 1

Estimate.

> Is the orange more than, less than, or about the same as 1 kilogram?

Step 2

Measure.

> The orange is up. It is less than 1 kilogram.

Complete the table.
Write **more than**, **less than**, or **about**.

	Object	Estimate	Measure
1.	apple	_____ 1 gram	_____ 1 gram
2.	math book	_____ 1 kilogram	_____ 1 kilogram
3.	pair of shoes	_____ 1 kilogram	_____ 1 kilogram

Write **more than**, **less than**, or **about**.

	Object	Estimate	Measure
1.	dime	_____ 1 gram	_____ 1 gram
2.	spider	_____ 1 gram	_____ 1 gram
3.	crayon	_____ 1 gram	_____ 1 gram

Find objects that measure more than 1 kilogram.
Write their names in the table.
Use 1-kilogram objects and a balance scale to measure.

	Object	Estimate	Measure
4.	_____	about _____ kilograms	about _____ kilograms
5.	_____	about _____ kilograms	about _____ kilograms
6.	_____	about _____ kilograms	about _____ kilograms
7.	_____	about _____ kilograms	about _____ kilograms

8. List the objects in order from least to most kilograms.

_____ kg   _____ kg   _____ kg   _____ kg

 At Home Have your child search for food packages that might weigh about a kilogram (kg).

Writing Math: Create and Solve

Draw an object that is less than 10 kilograms on the balance. Tell how many kilograms it is.

Use the shapes below to show the number of kilograms for the object you choose.

Draw the shapes on the other side of the balance.

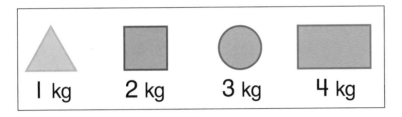

| 1 kg | 2 kg | 3 kg | 4 kg |

My object is _____ .

The object is about_____ kilograms.

Quick Check

Circle the one that holds more.

1. 3 cups   1 pint

3. 1 quart   3 pints

2. 1 gallon   3 quarts

4. 4 cups   1 gallon

Think about how much the object holds.
Circle the better estimate.

5.

10 milliliters   10 liters

6.

40 milliliters   40 liters

Think about how much it weighs.
Write **more than**, **less than**, or **about**.

7.

_____ 1 pound

8.

_____ 1 ounce

Think about how heavy the object is.
Write **more than**, **less than**, or **about**.

9.

_____ 1 kilogram

10.

_____ 1 gram

Temperature: Fahrenheit

You can use a **thermometer** to measure **temperature** in **degrees Fahrenheit (°F)**.

From one line to the next the temperature changes 2 degrees.

Count up by 2s from 80° to the top of the red bar.

80°, 82°, 84°

The temperature is 84°F.

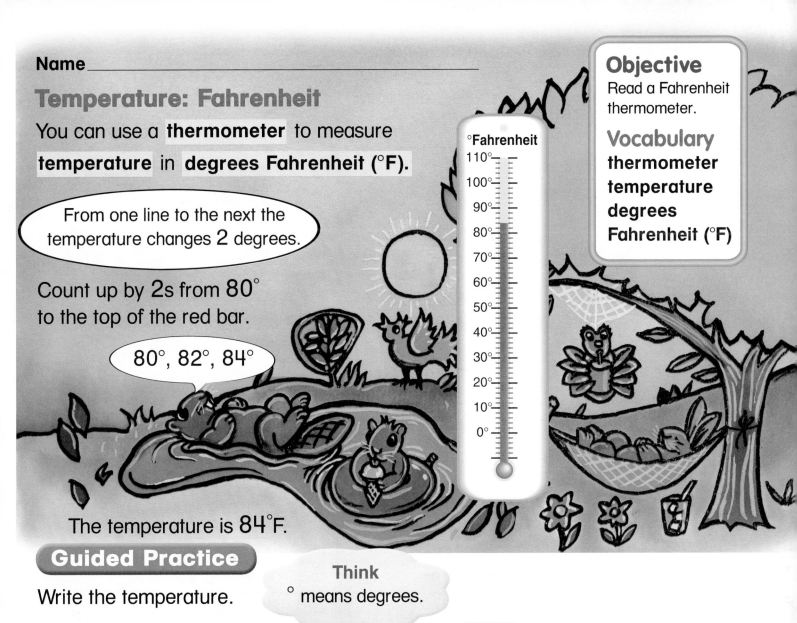

Objective
Read a Fahrenheit thermometer.

Vocabulary
thermometer
temperature
degrees
Fahrenheit (°F)

Guided Practice

Write the temperature.

Think
° means degrees.

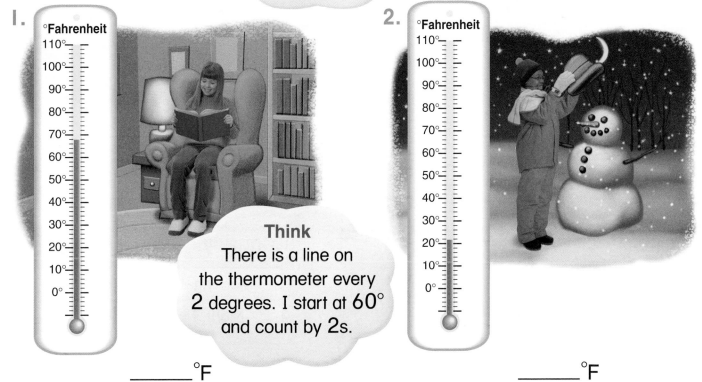

Think
There is a line on the thermometer every 2 degrees. I start at 60° and count by 2s.

1. _____°F

2. _____°F

TEST TIPS **Explain Your Thinking** Why do we say the temperature goes up or down?

Remember
From one line to the next is **2** degrees.

Write the temperature.

1.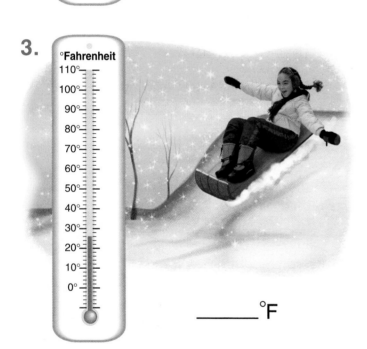

_58_ °F

2. °Fahrenheit
110°
100°
90°
80°
70°
60°
50°
40°
30°
20°
10°
0°

_____ °F

3. °Fahrenheit
110°
100°
90°
80°
70°
60°
50°
40°
30°
20°
10°
0°

_____ °F

4. °Fahrenheit
110°
100°
90°
80°
70°
60°
50°
40°
30°
20°
10°
0°

_____ °F

Problem Solving ▶ Data Sense

Use the table to answer the question.

5. How many degrees did the temperature change from the morning to the night? _____ °F

6. At noon the temperature was 75°F. Did the temperature go up or down since morning? _____

Monday's Temperatures	
Morning	70°F
Night	50°F

 At Home Help your child get the temperature forecast for tomorrow. Discuss if it will be hot, warm, cool, or cold and what he or she should wear to go outside.

Temperature: Celsius

Some thermometers measure temperature in **degrees Celsius (°C).**

From one line to the next the temperature changes 5 degrees.

The temperature is 5° Celsius.

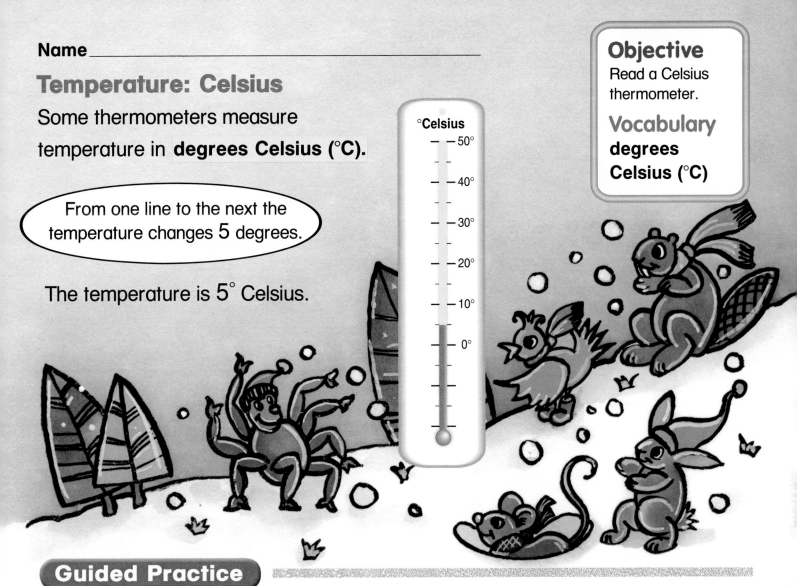

Guided Practice

Write the temperature.

1. _____ °C

Think
There is a line on the thermometer every 5 degrees.

2. _____ °C

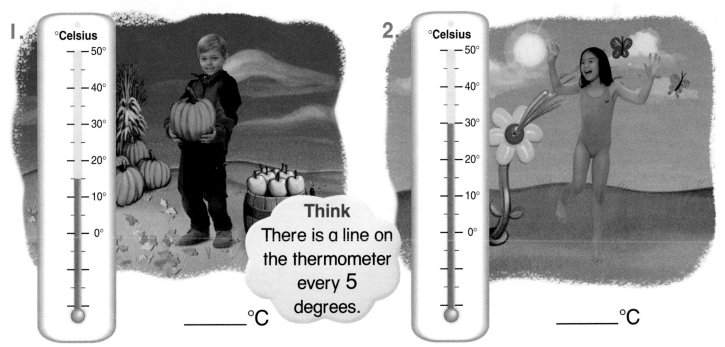

TEST TIPS **Explain Your Thinking** Is a temperature below 0°C warmer or colder than a temperature above 0°C? How do you know?

Remember
From one line to the next the temperature changes 5 degrees.

Write the temperature.

1.

°Celsius

__25__ °C

2.

°Celsius

_____ °C

3.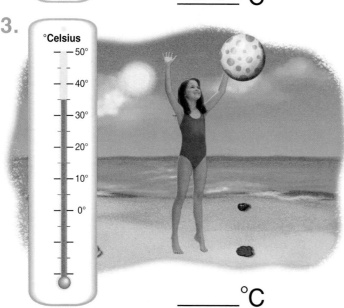

°Celsius

_____ °C

4.

°Celsius

_____ °C

Problem Solving ▶ Measurement Sense

Shade to show the temperature.

5. 5°C

°Celsius

6. 30°C

°Celsius

At Home Have your child describe the scenes and temperatures on this page as cold, cool, warm, or hot.

Measuring Units and Tools

You use different units and different tools to measure.

Inch
Centimeter

how long or tall

Cup
Liter

how much

Pound
Kilogram

how heavy

°F   °C

how warm
or cold

Guided Practice

Circle the unit used to measure.
Then circle the correct tool.

Think
Which unit is used to measure weight?

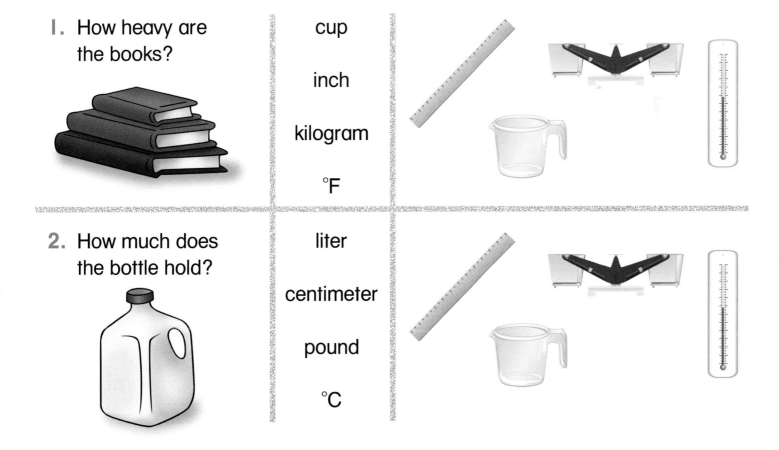

1. How heavy are
   the books?

cup

inch

kilogram

°F

2. How much does
   the bottle hold?

liter

centimeter

pound

°C

TEST TIPS **Explain Your Thinking** Which units and tools would you use to find the length of a piece of string? Tell why.

Think about what
you are being asked
to measure.

Circle the unit needed to measure.
Then circle the correct tool.

1. How long is the leaf?

liter

(inch)

pound

°F

2. What is the temperature?

liter

foot

pound

°C

3. How heavy is the bag
of peaches?

cup

centimeter

pound

°C

4. How much does the
pail hold?

cup

inch

kilogram

°F

Problem Solving ▶ Measurement Sense

Look at the object. Circle what you can measure. Explain.

5.

how warm

how tall

how long

how much

6.

how warm

how heavy

how long

how much

At Home Ask your child which tool he or she would use to answer
each question. How heavy is the book? How tall are you? How warm is
it outside? How much water is in the bowl?

Name _____

Reasonable Answers

 MathTracks 2/27
Listen and Understand

Problem Solving

Objective
Determine if a measure is reasonable.

Mr. Donald's class walks to the park.
They collect things to measure.

Choose the most reasonable answer.

Luis is looking at leaves.
He finds a gold leaf.

About how long could the leaf be?

5 feet    5 inches   5 pounds

THINK

DECIDE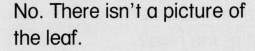

Do I need to measure the leaf?

No. There isn't a picture of the leaf.

What should I use to solve the problem?

I can use what I know about ways to measure and leaves.

Which unit is reasonable?

I know pounds measure weight not length.

5 feet is too long.

5 inches makes the most sense.

The gold leaf could be about 5 inches long.

Guided Practice

Circle the most reasonable answer.

1. Lena plants a tree that is 1 foot tall. The tree grows a little each week. About how tall is the tree after 5 weeks?

   Think
   1 foot equals 12 inches, so 10 inches is too short.

   Draw or write to explain.

   10 inches   (15 inches)   10 feet

2. Ten children take 1 gallon of lemonade to drink on a hike. They drink almost all of it. About how much lemonade is left after the hike?

   Think
   The children like lemonade. 5 gallons is more than they took.

   5 ounces   5 pints   5 gallons

Practice

3. Mr. Donald's class wears jackets on their spring hike. He records the temperature at lunchtime. What is the temperature?

   25°F   65°F   95°F

4. Bev fills a bag with pebbles. She carries the bag in her pocket. How much does the bag of pebbles weigh?

   2 pounds 35 pounds 100 pounds

At Home Ask your child to create a similar problem about something he or she finds in or around the home. Then have your child explain the most reasonable answer.

Quick Check

Write the temperature.

1.

_____°F

2.

_____°C

Circle the unit needed to measure.
Then circle the correct tool.

3. How heavy is the pineapple?

liter

inch

pound

°C

4. How tall is the doll?

cup

centimeter

kilogram

°F

Circle the most reasonable answer.

5. Jake reads the thermometer in his classroom. What is the temperature?

Draw or write to explain.

28°F   44°F   72°F

Subtract.

1. 80
   − 7

2. 94
   −62

3. 87
   −18

4. 63
   −27

5. 75
   −39

6. 34
   −15

7. 64
   −35

8. 92
   −73

9. 56
   −18

10. 24
    − 7

11. 31
    −26

12. 74
    −34

13. 83
    −48

14. 37
    −19

15. 71
    −43

Rewrite the numbers. Subtract.

16. 47 − 16

Tens	Ones

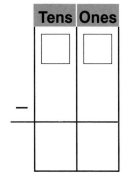

17. 99 − 98

Tens	Ones

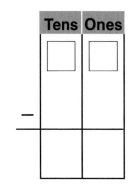

18. 96 − 49

Tens	Ones

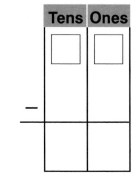

19. 81 − 37

Tens	Ones

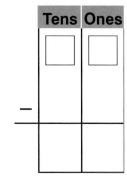

Science Connection   **Jumping Animals**

Some animals can jump higher than a person!

Look at the table. List the jumps from least to greatest.

High Jump	
Horse	9 feet
Person	8 feet
Kangaroo	10 feet

_____ _____ _____

WEEKLY WR READER eduplace.com/kids/mw/

Vocabulary (*e* • Glossary)

Complete the sentence.

| kilograms |
| thermometer |
| liter |

1. A _____ measures the temperature.

2. You can use _____ to measure how heavy an object is.

3. A water bottle holds about 1 _____ of water.

Concepts and Skills

Circle which holds more.

4. 2 gallons or 1 quart

5. 3 cups or 1 pint

Think about how much the object holds.
Circle the better estimate.

6.

120 L   120 mL

7.

25 mL   25 L

Think about how much it weighs.
Write **more than**, **less than**, or **about**.

8.

_____ a pound

9.

_____ a pound

Think about how heavy the object is.
Write **more than**, **less than**, or **about**.

10.

_____ a kilogram

11.

_____ a kilogram

Write the temperature.

12.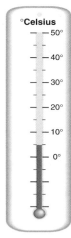

_____ °F

13.

_____ °C

Circle the unit used to measure.
Then circle the correct tool.

14. How heavy is the
bunch of grapes?

liter

meter

pound

°C

Problem Solving

Circle the most reasonable answer.

Draw or write to explain.

15. Tara brings a gallon of water
to soccer practice. She
shares most of it with her
friends. How much does she
have left after practice?

10 ounces   10 pints   10 gallons

530 five hundred thirty

Name

Highland Games

About 200 years ago, the Highland Games were started in Scotland. Today, the games are held in many places, including Tulsa, Oklahoma. These games test people's strength. One event is the Caber Toss. A caber is a wooden pole that looks like a telephone pole. It can weigh between 100 and 150 pounds.

People flip a caber like this.

Draw or write to explain.

1. Glen tosses a caber that is 15 feet long. James tosses a caber that is 22 feet long.

   Who tosses the longer caber? How much longer is it?

   _____

   _____ feet

2. Saturday 50 people do the Caber Toss. Sunday 48 people do the Caber Toss. How many people do the Caber Toss in all?

   _____ people

3. Drew makes a new caber. It is now 22 feet long. He wants it to be 20 feet. How many feet of wood does he need to cut off?

   _____ feet

4. The first Caber Toss starts at 10:00 A.M. The event ends at 4:00 P.M. How long does the event last?

   _____ hours

Some other events in the Highland Games are the Hammer Throw, the Weight Throw, and the Shot-Put. In the Shot-Put, people make 3 throws.

These tables show the results of some events in the Highland Games.

Use the tables to solve.

Hammer Throw	
Person	Distance
George	75 ft
Chris	50 ft

Weight Throw	
Person	Distance
Kate	28 ft
Meg	24 ft

Shot-Put	
Person	Distance
Karl	32 ft
Malcolm	29 ft

1. How much farther does George throw the hammer than Chris?

Draw or write to explain.

_____ feet

2. How many fewer feet does Meg throw the weight than Kate?

_____ feet

3. Karl and Malcom each throw the shot-put 3 times. Who throws the shot-put the greater total distance?

_____

4. How much farther does Chris throw the hammer than Meg throws the weight?

_____ feet

Technology

Visit *Education Place* at
eduplace.com/kids/mw/
to learn more about this topic.

Name _____

Vocabulary (*e* • Glossary)

Complete the sentence.

| pint |
| kilogram |
| perimeter |
| thermometer |

1. The distance around a plane shape
   is its _____.

2. Two cups hold a _____ of liquid.

3. A _____ measures temperature.

4. You use a _____ to measure
   how heavy an object is.

Concepts and Skills

Circle the better estimate.

5.

   12 inches   5 inches

6.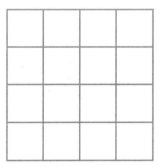

   30 centimeters   12 centimeters

Find the perimeter and area.

7. _____ + _____ + _____ + _____ = _____ cm.

   The perimeter is about _____ centimeters.

   The area is about _____ square centimeters.

Write the number that makes each sentence true.

8. 2 pints = _____ cups   4 quarts = _____ gallon

Unit 7 Test

Circle the better estimate.

9.

2 milliliters   **2 liters**

10.

20 milliliters   **20 liters**

Write the temperature.

11.

_____ °F

12.

_____ °C

Circle the unit needed to measure.
Then circle the correct tool.

13. How tall is
    the doll?

liter

pound

inch

Problem Solving

Use the picture to solve the problem.

14. Ingrid draws a border around
    the picture. How long will the
    border be?

Draw or write to explain.

3 cm

2 cm

_____ cm

Circle the most reasonable answer.

15. It is a hot summer day at
    the beach.

95°F   52°F   32°F

534 five hundred thirty-four

Name ____________________

Performance Assessment

1. Draw a shape with an area that is 4 square units.

Show your work with pictures, numbers, or words.

2. Draw 2 different shapes each with an area of 6 square units.

Show your work with pictures, numbers, or words.

3. Isabel uses the lines on the grid to make a shape with yarn. Her shape has a perimeter of 10 centimeters. Show two shapes she can make.

Show your work with pictures, numbers, or words.

_____

Name_____

Estimate Volume

Volume tells how many unit cubes are in an object.

Some objects have a larger volume than others. A bathtub has a very large volume, while a cup has a rather small volume.

Read exercises below. Find the volume of these objects by counting the cubes.

1. How many cubes are in this figure?

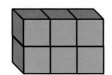

_____ cubes

2. How many cubes are in this figure?

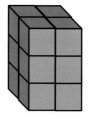

_____ cubes

Estimate.

3. Jay works at a toy store. He needs to pack these cubes in boxes. About how many cubes do you think will fit in each box?

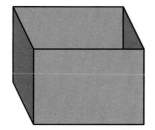

about _____ cubes

4. Alba built these castles for her little brother. Which castle has a greater volume —A or B?

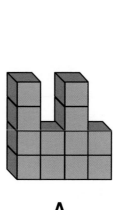 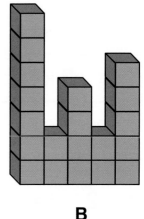

A   B

castle _____

Technology
Visit *Education Place* at
eduplace.com/kids/mw/
for brain teasers.

Calculator
Measurement Patterns

There are 2 cups in 1 pint. How many cups are in 5 pints?

Use a calculator.

Find the number of cups in 5 pints.

Press: 2 + 2 = 4

Each time you press = , 2 more will be added.

Press: = = = 10

There are 10 cups in 5 pints.

Use a calculator to finish each table.

1.

1 foot	2 feet	3 feet	4 feet	5 feet
12 inches	_____ inches	_____ inches	_____ inches	_____ inches

2.

1 yard	2 yards	3 yards	4 yards	5 yards
3 feet	_____ feet	_____ feet	_____ feet	_____ feet

Circle the greater amount.

3. 12 inches   2 feet

4. 2 pints   2 cups

5. 3 yards   12 feet

6. 4 feet   24 inches

Test-Taking Tips
. . . .

Read each question twice before
you answer it.

Check each answer twice.

Multiple Choice

Fill in the ○ for the correct answer.

1. About how long is this pencil?

2 cm	7 cm	15 cm	30 cm
○	○	○	○

2. Which measurement below
is the longest?

3 ft	3 in.	1 ft	9 in.
○	○	○	○

3. Which is the best unit to tell how
much water is in a bathtub?

cup	pint	quart	gallon
○	○	○	○

4. Subtract.

$$\begin{array}{r} 65 \\ -\ 18 \\ \hline \end{array}$$

47	37	33	29
○	○	○	○

Multiple Choice

Fill in the ○ for the correct answer. NH means Not Here.

5. About how much water does a teaspoon hold?

I liter   2 liters

○   ○

10 milliliters   NH

○   ○

6. What is the temperature?

66°F   72°F

○   ○

82°F   NH

○   ○

7. Which unit of measure would you use to tell how much a pumpkin weighs?

cups   inches   pounds   NH

○   ○   ○   ○

Open Response

Solve.

8. What is the value of these coins?

_____

9. Paco goes to soccer practice at 3:00. He comes home at 5:00. How long is he at soccer practice?

_____ hours

10. Kay puts ribbon around this picture frame. How much ribbon does she need?

5 cm

10 cm

_____

Test Prep on the Net
Visit *Education Place* at
eduplace.com/kids/mw/
for more test prep practice.

Numbers and Operations Through 1,000, Multiplication, and Division

From the
Read-Aloud Anthology

The Queen's Key

illustrated by Bob Barner

Access Prior Knowledge

This poem will help you review

- Two-digit addition and subtraction
- Skip counting
- Place value

541b from *The Queen's Key*

Miss Bee is in charge of the special key
That opens the chest of the royal honey.
The queen needs the key to give her honey a taste.
She calls up Miss Bee, but the key is misplaced!
Oh, no! She left the key at Aunt Bee's house one day.
She needs all her friends to help her along the way.

Her Aunt grabs the key and heads for the door.
She drives 50 miles, then 7 miles more,
Before her car breaks down at Mr. Ant's door!
Aunt Bee begs Mr. Ant, "Please, we can't quit.
Take this key to the queen, lickety-split."

Mr. Ant grabs the key and jumps in his boat.
He rows with both oars and soon is afloat.
He rows 40 miles, then 12 miles more,
When his boat springs a leak near Mr. Spider's door.
"Help me Mr. Spider, we have to keep going!
Take this key from my arms which are worn out from
rowing."

Spider grabs the key and straps on his skates.
He needs all four pairs for each of his legs!
He skates 60 miles, then 10 miles more,
Then his skate loses a wheel at Ms. Ladybug's door.
Ms. Ladybug sees the key and knows what to do.
She hops in her plane that is shiny and new.

She steers her plane past stars and the sun
Then lands at the castle, the journey is done!
The queen takes the key from her friend Ladybug.
She shouts for joy and gives her a hug.
She gives presents to all of Miss Bee's friends,
Everyone is happy, so this is THE END!

Unit 8

Name _____

Use the poem on page 541c.
Solve.

Draw or write to explain.

1. How many miles in all did each character travel with the key?

Aunt Bee _____ miles

Mr. Ant _____ miles

Mr. Spider _____ miles

2. Use the clues to find the number of miles Ms. Ladybug traveled.
   · The ones digit is one more than 5.
   · The tens digit is 2 more than the ones digit.

_____ _____ miles
tens   ones

3. Each of Mr. Spider's skates has 5 wheels. How many wheels are there in all? Skip count to find the answer.

_____ wheels

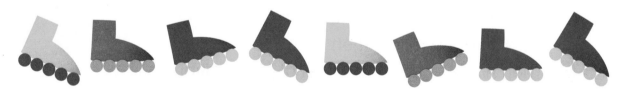

____ ____ ____ ____ ____ ____ ____ ____

4. **Create Your Own** Write your own clues for the number of miles Aunt Bee traveled in all. Write the number.

· The ones digit is _____

· The tens digit is _____

_____ _____ miles
tens   ones

Dear Family,

My class is starting Unit 8. I will be learning about numbers through 1,000, multiplication, and division. These pages show some of what I will learn and have activities for us to do together.

From, _____

Vocabulary

These are some words I will use in this unit.

multiply

3 x 2 = 6

↑ number of groups   ↑ number in each group   ↑ number in all

divide

6 ÷ 3 = 2

↑ number in all   ↑ number of groups   ↑ number in each group

product

3 x 2 = 6
↑ product

```
    2
  x 3
    6
```
product ⟶ 6

division sentence

15 ÷ 5 = 3

15 divided by 5 equals 3.

multiplication sentence

2 x 5 = 10

2 times 5 equals 10.

hundred

100 = 1 hundred

10 tens = 1 hundred

Some other words I will use are **digit**, **place value**, **regroup**, **dollar sign**, and **decimal point.**

Vocabulary Activity

Turn the page for more.

Let's work together to complete these sentences.

1. In 3 x 3 = 9, the number 9 is the _____.

2. 8 ÷ 4 = 2 is an example of a _____.

3. 10 tens is the same as a _____.

How To subtract three-digit numbers

In this unit, I will be learning about adding and subtracting. This three-digit subtraction problem is an example of what I will be learning.

Subtract 336 – 172.

Step 1

Show 336.

Subtract the ones.

Workmat 6		
Hundreds	**Tens**	**Ones**

H	T	O
3	3	6
– 1	7	2

Step 2

Regroup 1 hundred as 10 tens.

Subtract the tens.

Workmat 6		
Hundreds	**Tens**	**Ones**

H	T	O
2	13	
3	3	6
– 1	7	2
	6	4

Step 3

Subtract the hundreds.

Workmat 6		
Hundreds	**Tens**	**Ones**

H	T	O
2	13	
3	3	6
– 1	7	2
	6	4

📘 Literature

These books link to the math in this unit. We can look for them at the library.

Amanda Bean's Amazing Dream
Story by Cindy Neuschwander
Math activities by Marilyn Burns
Pictures by Lisa Woodruff
(Scholastic Press, 1998)

Moira's Birthday
Story by Robert Munsch

Technology

We can visit *Education Place* at **eduplace.com/parents/mw/** for the Math Lingo game, the *e* Glossary, and more games and activities to do together.

Multiplication and Division

CHAPTER 19

INVESTIGATION

What equal groups do you see at this pond?

Counting Critters

Listen to each bug story.
Use counters to act out each story.

Name_____

Activity: Exploring Multiplication

 **MathTracks 2**/28
Listen and Understand

When all the groups have the same
number they are **equal groups.**

Objective
Relate equal groups,
repeated addition, and skip
counting to multiplication.

Vocabulary
equal groups

I add to find
how many in all.

Work Together

Take turns doing each step.

1. Make equal groups with counters.
2. Complete the addition sentence.

	Number of Equal Groups	Number in Each Group	How Many in All?
1.	4	2	2 + 2 + 2 + 2 = 8
2.	2	5	___ + ___ = ___
3.	3	4	___ + ___ + ___ = ___
4.	5	3	___ + ___ + ___ + ___ + ___ = ___
5.	5	2	___ + ___ + ___ + ___ + ___ = ___

Work Together

There are 3 groups of 2. How many in all?
There are many ways to find an answer.

You can use the number line to skip count.

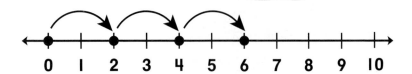

2, 4, 6

0 1 2 3 4 5 6 7 8 9 10

You can add equal groups.

$$2 + 2 + 2 = 6$$

Use a number line or add equal groups.
Write the answer.

1. 2 groups of 3

2. 3 groups of 5

_____

_6_

On Your Own

3. 2 groups of 4

_____

4. 3 groups of 3

_____

5. 2 groups of 10

6. 4 groups of 3

_____

7. **Talk About It** How are skip counting and addition alike?

At Home Use dry cereal or pasta to make equal groups of 5.
Ask your child to find the total number of items.

548 five hundred forty-eight

Multiply With 2 and 5

 MathTracks 2/29
Listen and Understand

Add equal groups to find the sum.
Multiply equal groups to find the **product.**

3 groups of 2

> 3 times 2 equals 6.

Add.
$2 + 2 + 2 =$ ___6___
↑
sum

Multiply.

| 3 | × | 2 | = | ___6___ |

↑ number of groups   ↑ number in each group   ↑ product

$3 × 2 = 6$ is a **multiplication sentence.**

Guided Practice

Find the sum.
Then find the product.

> **Think**
> $5 + 5 + 5$ is the same as $3 × 5$.

1. 3 groups of 5

$5 + 5 + 5 =$ ___15___
$3 × 5 =$ ___15___

2. 2 groups of 2

$2 + 2 =$ _____
$2 × 2 =$ _____

3. 6 groups of 5

$5 + 5 + 5 + 5 + 5 + 5 =$ _____

$6 × 5 =$ _____

TEST TIPS **Explain Your Thinking** How does skip counting help you find the product?

Remember that you can skip count to find the product.

Find the sum.
Then find the product.

1. 3 groups of 2

2 + 2 + 2 = _____

3 × 2 = _____

2. 4 groups of 5

5 + 5 + 5 + 5 = _____

4 × 5 = _____

3. 5 groups of 5

5 + 5 + 5 + 5 + 5 = _____

5 × 5 = _____

4. 5 groups of 2

2 + 2 + 2 + 2 + 2 = _____

5 × 2 = _____

5. 3 × 5 = _____

6. 9 × 2 = _____

7. 10 × 2 = _____

8. 8 × 5 = _____

9. 7 × 2 = _____

10. 9 × 5 = _____

Problem Solving ▶ Number Sense

11. Multistep Jen has 2 baskets. There are 3 apples in each basket. She needs 7 apples to make a pie. Can Jen make a pie?

Draw or write to explain.

Yes   No

At Home Use small objects to make groups of 2 and groups of 5. Ask your child to write multiplication sentences to show how many in all.

Multiply With 10

There are 10 cubes in each cube train.
How many cubes are in 5 trains?

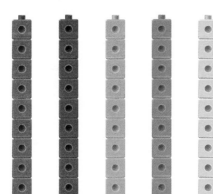

_____5 tens_____

__5__ × 10 = __50__

I can skip count by 10s.
10, 20, 30, 40, 50.

Guided Practice

Write how many 10s.
Multiply.

Think
I skip count by 10s.

1. 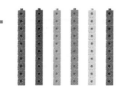 _____ tens   6 × 10 = _____

2. _____ tens   4 × 10 = _____

3. _____ tens   2 × 10 = _____

4.  _____ tens   8 × 10 = _____

TEST TIPS **Explain Your Thinking** How can you use multiplication to find the value of 8 dimes?

Write how many 10s.
Multiply.

1.

Remember to skip count by 10s.

_____1_____ ten   1 × 10 = __10__

2.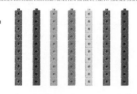

_____ tens   3 × 10 = _____

3.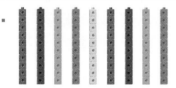

_____ tens   7 × 10 = _____

4.

_____ tens   9 × 10 = _____

Multiply.

5. 2 × 10 = _____   6. 6 × 10 = _____   7. 6 × 5 = _____

8. 8 × 5 = _____   9. 7 × 2 = _____   10. 2 × 5 = _____

Problem Solving ▶ Visual Thinking

11. Draw 3 sets of 10.

12. Write a multiplication sentence for the picture.

13. Circle the product.

Draw or write to explain.

_____ ◯ _____ = _____

 **At Home** Practice multiplying numbers by 2, 5, and 10 with your child.

Multiply in Any Order

MathTracks 2/30
Listen and Understand

You can multiply in any order and get the same product.

When I turn the paper, the product is the same.

5 rows of 3

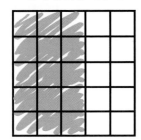

3 rows of 5

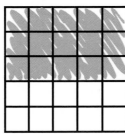

$5 \times 3 =$ __15__ $3 \times 5 =$ __15__

Guided Practice

Color to make equal rows. Find the product.

Think
I can multiply 2 and 5 in either order. The product is the same.

1. 2 rows of 5   5 rows of 2

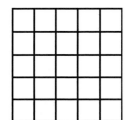   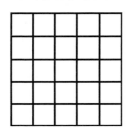

$2 \times 5 =$ ____ $5 \times 2 =$ ____

2. 3 rows of 5   5 rows of 3

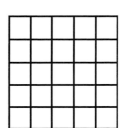   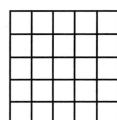

$3 \times 5 =$ ____ $5 \times 3 =$ ____

3. 2 rows of 3   3 rows of 2

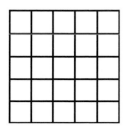   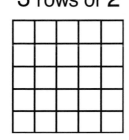

$2 \times 3 =$ ____ $3 \times 2 =$ ____

4. 4 rows of 2   2 rows of 4

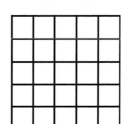   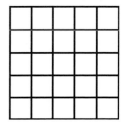

$4 \times 2 =$ ____ $2 \times 4 =$ ____

TEST TIPS **Explain Your Thinking** How is 5×4 the same as 4×5?

The order of the numbers does not change the product.

Color to make equal rows. Find the product.

1. 2 rows of 2   2 rows of 2

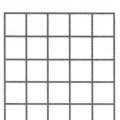 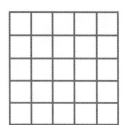

$2 \times 2 = \underline{\quad4\quad}$ $2 \times 2 = \underline{\quad4\quad}$

2. 4 rows of 5   5 rows of 4

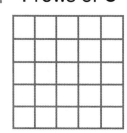 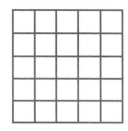

$4 \times 5 = \underline{\qquad}$ $5 \times 4 = \underline{\qquad}$

3. 5 rows of 2   2 rows of 5

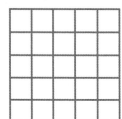 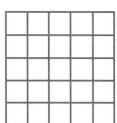

$5 \times 2 = \underline{\qquad}$ $2 \times 5 = \underline{\qquad}$

4. 5 rows of 5   5 rows of 5

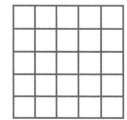 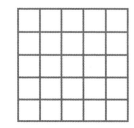

$5 \times 5 = \underline{\qquad}$ $5 \times 5 = \underline{\qquad}$

Multiply.

5. $2 \times 9 = \underline{\qquad}$ $9 \times 2 = \underline{\qquad}$

6. $6 \times 5 = \underline{\qquad}$ $5 \times 6 = \underline{\qquad}$

7. $7 \times 2 = \underline{\qquad}$ $2 \times 7 = \underline{\qquad}$

8. $6 \times 2 = \underline{\qquad}$ $2 \times 6 = \underline{\qquad}$

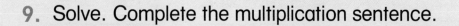

Algebra Readiness ▶ Properties

9. Solve. Complete the multiplication sentence.

If $3 \times 5 = \underline{\qquad}$,   then $5 \times 3 = \underline{\qquad}$.

If $2 \times \underline{\qquad} = 10$,   then $5 \times \underline{\qquad} = 10$.

If $\underline{\qquad} \times 3 = 6$,   then $\underline{\qquad} \times 2 = 6$.

At Home Have your child solve multiplication problems such as 4×2 and 2×4. Ask him or her to explain why the product is the same.

Name _____

Writing Math: Create and Solve

Draw equal groups of fish in a pond.

Write a multiplication story about the fish in a pond.

_____

_____

_____

_____

_____

Write a multiplication sentence to solve your problem.

_____ × _____ = _____

Share your multiplication story.

Quick Check

Make equal groups of counters.
Draw the counters.
Complete the addition sentence.

1. 2 groups of 3   _____ + _____ = _____

Find the sum.
Then find the product.

2. 3 groups of 5   _____ + _____ + _____ = _____

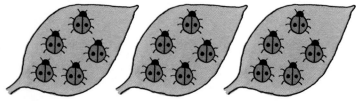   _____ × _____ = _____

Color to make equal rows.
Find the product.

3. 4 rows of 2   2 rows of 4   4. 5 rows of 2   2 rows of 5

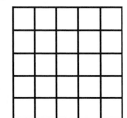   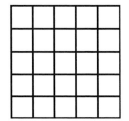   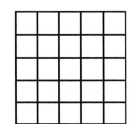   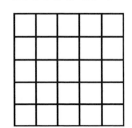

4 × 2 = _____   2 × 4 = _____   5 × 2 = _____   2 × 5 = _____

Multiply.

5. 2 × 8 = _____   6. 7 × 5 = _____

   8 × 2 = _____   5 × 7 = _____

7. 2 × 10 = _____   8. 6 × 10 = _____

Name_____

Activity: Share Equally

 MathTracks 2/31
Listen and Understand

There are 15 counters.
There are 5 children.
How many counters does each child get?

You can **divide** the counters into
equal groups.

Objective
Share counters to
make equal groups.

Vocabulary
divide

Hands-On

Step 1

Show the 15 counters.
Look at the first row of
the chart.

Workmat 1

Step 2

Make 5 groups.
Put a counter in each
group to share.

Step 3

Keep sharing until all
counters are placed.

15 divided into 5 groups is 3.
15 ÷ 5 = 3
Each child gets 3 counters.

Work Together

Use Workmat 1 and counters. Divide.

	Number of Counters	Number of Groups	Divide	Number in Each Group
1.	15	5	15 ÷ 5	3
2.	10	5	10 ÷ 5	____
3.	16	4	16 ÷ 4	____

4. **Talk About It** How could 4 children share 20 counters equally?

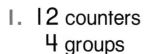

Use Workmat 1 and counters.
Draw dots to show the number in each group.
Write how many are in each group.

1. 12 counters
   4 groups

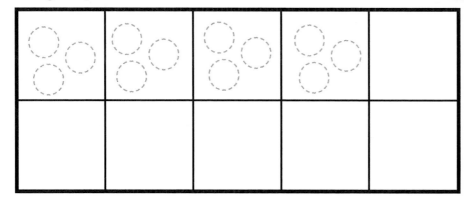

$12 \div 4 = \underline{\quad 3 \quad}$

$\underline{\quad 3 \quad}$ in each group

2. 16 counters
   8 groups

$16 \div 8 = \underline{\qquad}$

$\underline{\qquad}$ in each group

3. 20 counters
   5 groups

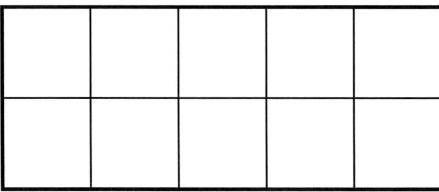

$20 \div 5 = \underline{\qquad}$

$\underline{\qquad}$ in each group

4. **Talk About It** When would you need to make equal groups?

At Home Have your child arrange 10 pennies into two equal groups.

Equal Groups of 2

How many groups of 2 can you make?

Step 1

Start with 10 bugs.

Step 2

Circle groups of 2.

Step 3

Write a **division sentence** to show how many equal groups there are.

$$\underline{10} \div \underline{2} = \underline{5}$$

__5__ equal groups

Guided Practice

Circle groups of 2.
Complete the division sentence.
Write the answer.

1.

Think
I see 6 fish.
I circle groups of 2 fish.

_____ ÷ _____ = _____

_____ equal groups

2.

_____ ÷ _____ = _____

_____ equal groups

3.

_____ ÷ _____ = _____

_____ equal groups

4.

_____ ÷ _____ = _____

_____ equal groups

TEST TIPS **Explain Your Thinking** What does the 2 mean in Exercise 3?

Remember that you are finding the number of groups.

Circle groups of 2.
Complete the division sentence.

1.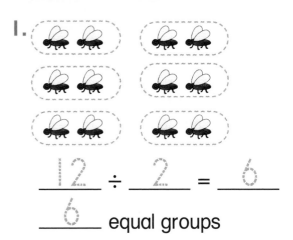

$\underline{12} \div \underline{2} = \underline{6}$

$\underline{6}$ equal groups

2.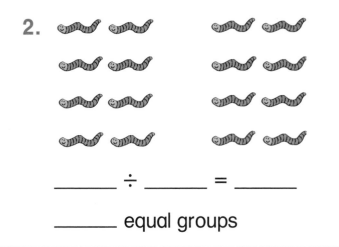

$\underline{} \div \underline{} = \underline{}$

$\underline{}$ equal groups

3.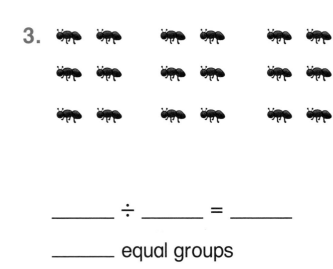

$\underline{} \div \underline{} = \underline{}$

$\underline{}$ equal groups

4.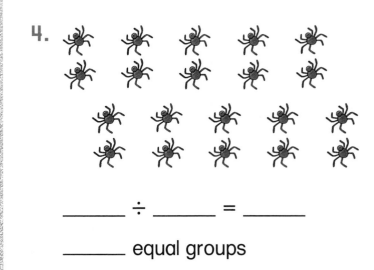

$\underline{} \div \underline{} = \underline{}$

$\underline{}$ equal groups

Problem Solving ▶ Reasoning

5. How many packs of seeds did Anthony use in the class garden?

_____ packs

6. How many packs of seeds did Christopher and Hope use in the class garden?

_____ packs

Packs of Seeds Used

Hope	🌸 🌸
Anthony	🌸 🌸 🌸 🌸
Christopher	🌸 🌸 🌸

Key: Each 🌸 stands for 2 packs

At Home Ask your child to divide 12 objects into equal groups of 2.

Equal Groups of 5

How many groups of 5 can you make?

Step 1

Start with 15 bees.

Step 2

Circle groups of 5.

Step 3

Write a division sentence to show how many groups there are.

____15____ ÷ ____5____ = ____3____

There are 3 groups of 5.

Guided Practice

Circle groups of 5.
Complete the division sentence.

1.

_____ ÷ _____ = _____

2.

_____ ÷ _____ = _____

3.

_____ ÷ _____ = _____

4.

_____ ÷ _____ = _____

TEST TIPS **Explain Your Thinking** Think about 5 + 5. Think about 2 × 5. How are they the same?

Remember to circle groups until there are no pictures left.

Circle groups of 5.
Complete the division sentence.

1.

   35 ÷ 5 = 7

2.

   _____ ÷ _____ = _____

3.

   _____ ÷ _____ = _____

4.

   _____ ÷ _____ = _____

Problem Solving ▶ Reasoning

5. Chantal has 15 jars of honey. She wants to share them equally among 5 people. Circle the picture that shows how she should divide.

  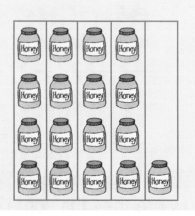

At Home Tell your child to imagine 20 children sitting in 4 equal groups. Ask him or her to write a division sentence that shows how many children are in each group.

Name_____

Draw a Picture

You can draw a picture to help you solve a problem.

Objective
Draw a picture to solve a problem.

Sim, Mateo, and Angela bring seeds for the class gardening project. Each child brings 5 seeds. How many seeds do the three children bring?

UNDERSTAND

What do you know?

- Three children bring seeds to school.
- Each child brings 5 seeds.

PLAN

You can draw a picture to solve.

- Do you need to find how many in all or how many each had? __how many in all__
- Do you multiply or divide? __multiply__

SOLVE

Draw a picture.

Use the picture to help you write a multiplication sentence.

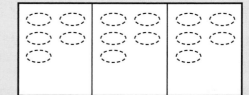

__3__ × __5__ = __15__

The children bring __15__ seeds.

LOOK BACK

- **Did you answer the question?**
- **How can you check your answer?**

Guided Practice

Draw a picture to solve.

Draw or write to explain.

1. There are 20 children in the class. They work in groups of 5 to study insects. How many groups will there be?

Think
I can draw 20 counters and circle groups of 5. Then I count the groups.

_____ groups

2. There are 2 teams. Each team brings in 9 flower pots. How many flower pots do they bring in?

Think
I can draw 2 groups of 9 each.

_____ flower pots

Practice

3. The class orders ants for their ant farm. They get 5 containers with the same number of ants in each. There are 25 ants in all. How many ants are in each container?

_____ ants

4. A group does a report on 4 plants on Monday. They report on 4 different plants on Tuesday. How many plants do they report on in all?

_____ plants

Go on

Name_____

Strategies

Draw a picture
Write a number sentence
Use models to act it out

Choose a Strategy

Solve.

1. Sharon has 5 flower pots. She plants 4 sunflowers in each pot. How many sunflowers does she plant?

Draw or write to explain.

sunflower

_____ sunflowers

2. Eli has 37 tulips. He plants the tulips in rows of 10. How many tulips are left over?

tulip

_____ tulips

3. Miss Singh picks 30 roses from her garden. She gives an equal number of roses to each of her 5 friends. How many roses does each friend get?

rose

_____ roses

4. **Multistep** Kayla has 8 daisies. She picks 8 more daisies. She gives a daisy to Matt, Cody, and Kelsea. How many daisies does Kayla have now?

daisy

_____ daisies

At Home Ask your child to explain how he or she knows whether to add, subtract, multiply, or divide to solve a problem.

Listen to your teacher read the problem.
Solve.

1. A bee has 4 wings. How many wings
do 5 bees have?

Show your work using
pictures, numbers, or words.

_____ wings

2. There are 50 seeds on the table.
If you make 5 equal groups, how
many seeds will be in each group?

_____ seeds

Listen to your teacher read the problem.
Choose the correct answer.

3.   2   5   7   35
      ○   ○   ○   ○

4.   2   10   20   25
      ○   ○   ○   ○

Use Workmat 1 and counters.
Draw dots to show the groups you make.
Write how many in each group.

1. 15 counters   5 groups

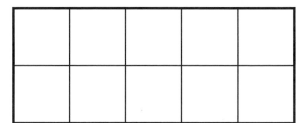

$15 \div 5 =$ _____

_____ in each group

2. 16 counters   8 groups

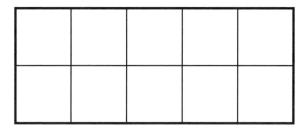

$16 \div 8 =$ _____

_____ in each group

Circle groups of 2.
Complete the division sentence.

3.

_____ $\div$ _____ = _____

Circle groups of 5.
Complete the division sentence.

4.

_____ $\div$ _____ = _____

Draw a picture to solve.

5. The queen bee wants to give
   Ant, Spider, and Ladybug each
   2 prizes. How many prizes does
   she need?

Draw or write to explain.

_____ prizes

Count on to find the total value of the coins.

1.

_____ ¢   _____ ¢   _____ ¢ _____ ¢   _____ ¢   _____ ¢
                                                        total

Use coins.
Draw two ways to make the amount.

2. 47¢

3. 47¢

Science Connection

Bees Knees

A bee has 6 legs. Each leg has 5 knees.
How many knees does a bee have?

_____ knees

How many more knees does
a bee have than you have?

_____ knees

Vocabulary   *e • Glossary*

Draw a line to match.

1. **equal groups**

2. **division sentence**

3. **product**

$14 \div 2 = 7$

the answer to a multiplication problem

the same number in each group

Concepts and Skills

Find the sum. Then find the product.

4. 3 groups of 5

$5 + 5 + 5 =$ _____

$3 \times 5 =$ _____

5. 5 groups of 2

$2 + 2 + 2 + 2 + 2 =$ _____

$5 \times 2 =$ _____

Write how many 10s. Multiply.

6. _____ tens

$6 \times 10 =$ _____

7. _____ tens

$8 \times 10 =$ _____

Color to make equal rows. Find the product.

8. 3 rows of 5   5 rows of 3

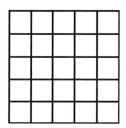

$3 \times 5 =$ _____ $5 \times 3 =$ _____

9. 5 rows of 2   2 rows of 5

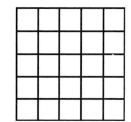   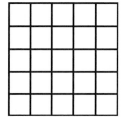

$5 \times 2 =$ _____ $2 \times 5 =$ _____

Multiply.

10. 8 × 2 = _____

2 × 8 = _____

11. 7 × 5 = _____

5 × 7 = _____

Circle groups of 2.
Complete the division sentence.
Write the answer.

12.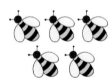

_____ ÷ _____ = _____

_____ groups

13.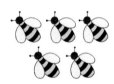

_____ ÷ _____ = _____

_____ groups

Circle groups of 5.
Complete the division sentence.

14.

_____ ÷ _____ = _____

Problem Solving

Draw a picture to solve.

Draw or write to explain.

15. There are 30 children at lunch. They sit in groups of 5 at each table. How many tables are there at lunch?

_____ tables

Numbers Through 1,000

INVESTIGATION

What numbers do you see?

Comparing Signs

Use  and ▫.

Make a number on the white sign.

Ask a friend if the number is greater than, less than, or equal to the number on the blue sign.

Name ________________________________

Hundreds and Tens

Objective
Count by hundreds and tens.

Vocabulary
hundreds

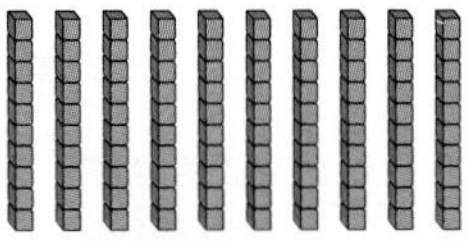
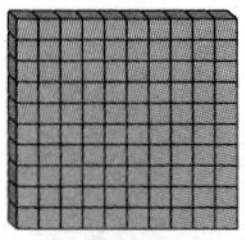

10 tens = 1 **hundred**
100

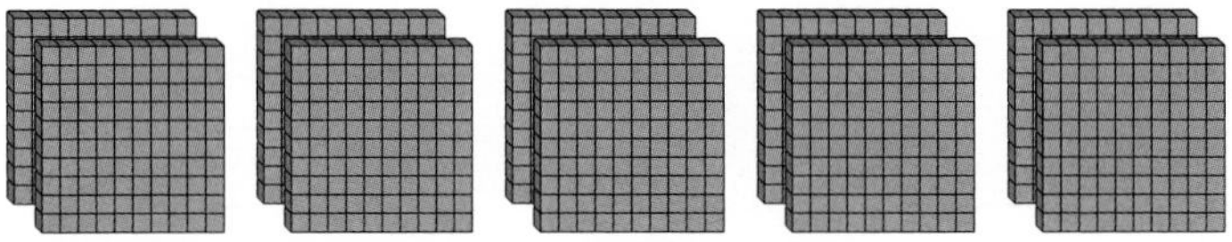
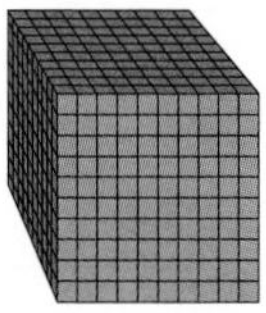

10 hundreds = 1 thousand
1,000

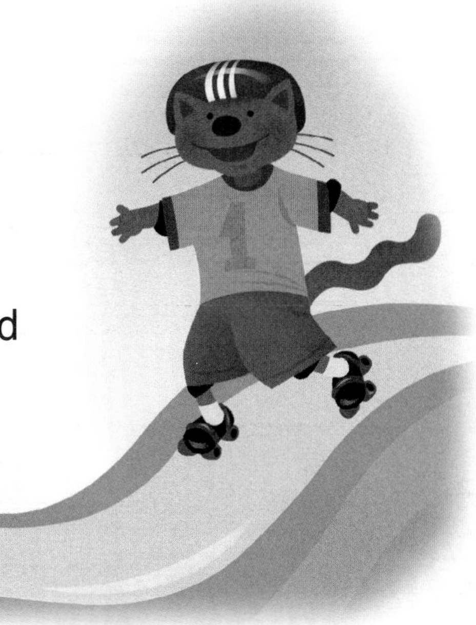

Guided Practice

Count by hundreds.
Write the number.

1. 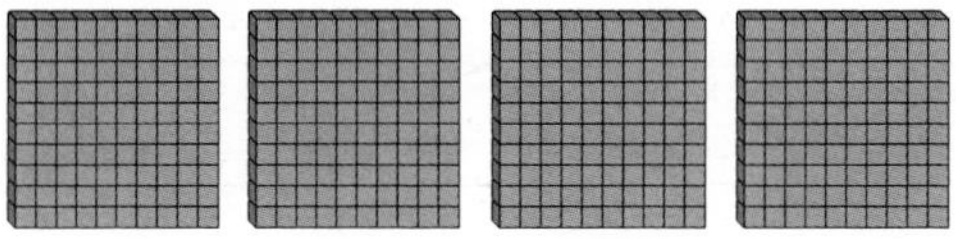

_____ hundreds ________
four hundred

Circle groups of tens.
Count by hundreds and tens.
Write the number.

2. 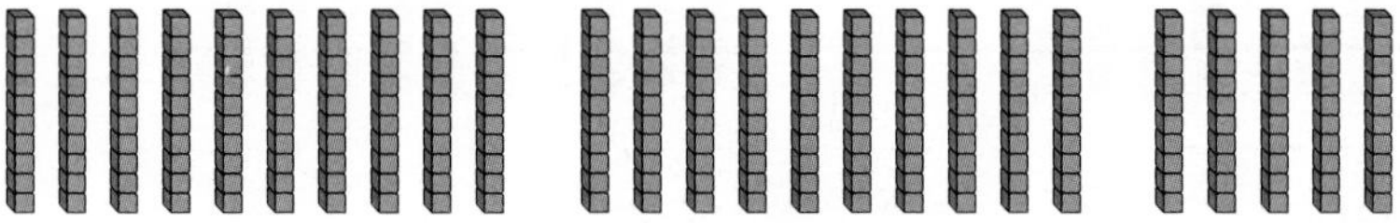

_____ hundreds _____ tens ________
two hundred fifty

Write the missing numbers.

3. 470 480 ______ 500 ______

TEST TIPS **Explain Your Thinking** How can you use skip counting to help you answer Exercise 3?

Remember
Count each 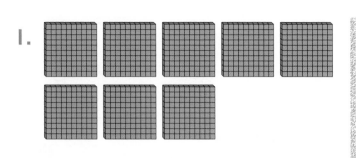 as 100.

Count by hundreds.
Write the number.

1. _____ hundreds   _____
eight hundred

2. _____ hundreds   _____
five hundred

3. _____ hundreds   _____
seven hundred

4. _____ hundreds   _____
one thousand

Circle groups of tens.
Count by hundreds and tens.
Write the number.

5. _____ hundreds   _____ tens

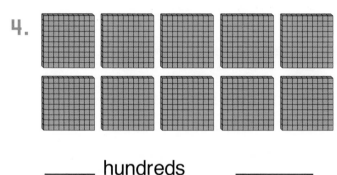

_____
three hundred ten

Write the missing numbers.

6. 100 200 _____ 400 _____ _____ 700 _____ 900 1,000

7. 1,000 900 _____ _____ 600 500 _____ _____ 200 _____

574 five hundred seventy-four

Go on

Count the hundreds and tens.
Write the number.

8.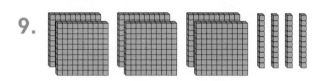

__2__ hundreds __3__ tens

Count by hundreds —
100, 200. Then count by
tens — 210, 220, 230.

__230__

two hundred thirty

9.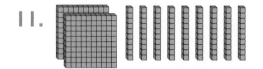

_____ hundreds _____ tens

_____ six hundred forty

10.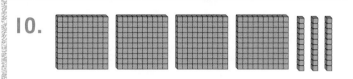

_____ hundreds _____ tens

_____ four hundred thirty

11.

_____ hundreds _____ tens

_____ two hundred ninety

12.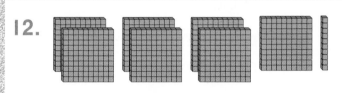

_____ hundreds _____ tens

_____ seven hundred ten

Problem Solving ▶ Number Sense

Complete the chart.
Write the numbers that are 100 more and 100 less.

	Start with	100 more	100 less
13.	354		
14.	865		
15.	218		

Chapter 20

At Home Ask your child to count forward by
hundreds from 100 to 1,000.

five hundred seventy-five **575**

SPIN A NUMBER

2 Players

What You Need: pencil, paper clip, tens and hundreds blocks, and Workmat 6

How to Play

1 Use a pencil and paper clip to set up the spinner.

2 Spin the spinner two times. Write both numbers.

3 Find the sum. Take that many tens.

4 Regroup 10 tens for 1 hundred if you can.

5 Write the hundreds and tens. Write the number.

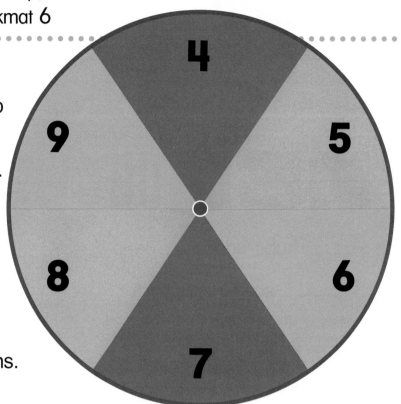

First spin	Second spin	Sum

_____ hundreds _____ tens _____

First spin	Second spin	Sum

_____ hundreds _____ tens _____

First spin	Second spin	Sum

_____ hundreds _____ tens _____

First spin	Second spin	Sum

_____ hundreds _____ tens _____

First spin	Second spin	Sum

_____ hundreds _____ tens _____

First spin	Second spin	Sum

_____ hundreds _____ tens _____

Name_____

Hundreds, Tens, and Ones

 MathTracks 2/32
Listen and Understand

Objective
Use models to show and count by hundreds, tens, and ones.

Hands-On

Show 134.

Workmat 6		
Hundreds	**Tens**	**Ones**

100 + 30 + 4 = 134

Think
1 hundred = 100
3 tens = 30
4 ones = 4

Hundreds	Tens	Ones
1	3	4

134

one hundred thirty-four

Guided Practice

Use Workmat 6 with ▨, ▭, and ▫.

Show the numbers with blocks.
Write how many.
Write the number.

Think
I count 6 hundreds, 4 tens, and 7 ones.

1. Show 6 ▨, 4 ▭, and 7 ▫.

Hundreds	Tens	Ones
6	4	7

647

2. Show 3 ▨, 5 ▭, and 2 ▫.

Hundreds	Tens	Ones

_____

3. Show 5 ▨, 7 ▭, and 6 ▫.

Hundreds	Tens	Ones

_____

TEST TIPS **Explain Your Thinking** Does the 3 in 163 have the same value as the 3 in 361? Explain.

Count hundreds first, then tens, and then ones.

Use Workmat 6 with , , and .

	Show this many.	Write how many.	Write the number.
1.		**Hundreds** 2 / **Tens** 4 / **Ones** 2	242 — two hundred forty-two
2.		**Hundreds** / **Tens** / **Ones**	_____ three hundred seventy-five
3.		**Hundreds** / **Tens** / **Ones**	_____ one hundred nine
4.		**Hundreds** / **Tens** / **Ones**	_____ eight hundred ten

Problem Solving ▶ Number Sense

Draw hundreds, tens, and ones to show each number.

5.	428	
6.	248	

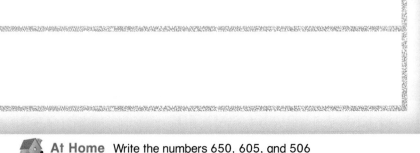

At Home Write the numbers 650, 605, and 506 and help your child say the numbers aloud.

Name _____

Identify Place Value to 1,000

Objective
Identify place
value to 1,000.

Vocabulary
digit

To find the value of a **digit,** find the value of its place.

Find the value of the digits in 257.

Hundreds	Tens	Ones
2	5	7

↓   ↓   ↓

200 + 50 + 7

↓

257

The 2 is in the hundreds place. Its value is 200.

The 5 is in the tens place. Its value is 50.

The 7 is in the ones place. Its value is 7.

Guided Practice

Write the number.

Think
I write 9 in the hundreds place, 6 in the tens place and 1 in the ones place.

1. 900 + 60 + 1 _____

2. 600 + 50 + 2 _____

3. 800 + 50 + 3 _____

4. 300 + 4 _____

5. 8 + 60 + 300 _____

6. 7 + 100 _____

Circle the value of the red digit.

7. | **849** |

800   80   8

8. | **962** |

600   60   6

9. | **294** |

400   40   4

TEST TIPS **Explain Your Thinking** What does the digit 0 in 704 mean?

Remember
To find the value of a digit, find the value of its place.

Write the number.

1. 1 + 20 + 300 ___321___

2. 4 + 80 + 200 _____

3. 6 + 800 _____

4. 7 + 60 _____

5. 3 + 10 + 400 _____

6. 600 + 30 + 2 _____

7. 7 + 50 + 800 _____

Circle the value of the red digit.

8. | 429 | (400)   40   4

9. | 781 | 800   80   8

10. | 352 | 300   30   3

11. | 527 | 200   20   2

12. | 637 | 700   70   7

13. | 409 | 900   90   9

Problem Solving ▶ Patterns

Count by 50. Write the missing numbers.

14. 100 150 200 250 _____ 350 _____ _____ 500

15. 600 650 700 750 _____ 850 900 _____ _____

At Home Write a three-digit number, such as 465 or 891. Have your child name the value of the digit in the tens place.

Read and Write Numbers Through 1,000

You can read and write numbers with words or symbols.

1 one	11 eleven	10 ten	100 one hundred
2 two	12 twelve	20 twenty	200 two hundred
3 three	13 thirteen	30 thirty	300 three hundred
4 four	14 fourteen	40 forty	400 four hundred
5 five	15 fifteen	50 fifty	500 five hundred
6 six	16 sixteen	60 sixty	600 six hundred
7 seven	17 seventeen	70 seventy	700 seven hundred
8 eight	18 eighteen	80 eighty	800 eight hundred
9 nine	19 nineteen	90 ninety	900 nine hundred
			1,000 one thousand

Guided Practice

Write the number.

1. eighty-five _____

2. fifty-four _____

3. three hundred seven _____

4. nine hundred twenty-one _____

Circle the word name for the number.

5. 78   seventy-eight   sixty-eight

6. 193   one-hundred thirty-nine   one hundred ninety-three

TEST TIPS **Explain Your Thinking** How do you know when to write a hyphen in a number word?

Remember
Read the number or number words to yourself to help you think of each part of the number.

Write the number.

1. seventy-one _____ 7/ _____   2. thirty-seven _____

3. fifteen _____   4. forty-three _____

5. twelve _____   6. ninety-eight _____

7. two hundred twenty-four _____   8. six hundred nine _____

9. five hundred fourteen _____   10. seven hundred thirty _____

Circle the word name for the number.

11. 27   (twenty-seven)   thirty-seven

12. 643   seven hundred forty-four   six hundred forty-three

13. 906   nine hundred six   nine hundred sixteen

14. 513   five hundred thirteen   fifty-three

15. 748   seven hundred forty-three   seven hundred forty-eight

16. 720   seven hundred twenty   seven hundred twelve

Problem Solving ▶ Data Sense

17. How many people were at the fair on Friday and Saturday?

_____ people

18. How many more people were at the fair on Saturday than on Sunday?

_____ people

People at the Fair	
Friday	🧍🧍
Saturday	🧍🧍🧍🧍🧍
Sunday	🧍🧍🧍🧍

Key: Each 🧍 stands for 100 people

At Home Write a three-digit number such as 475 and ask your child to write the number name in words.

Name ______________________________

Different Ways to Show Numbers

Objective
Use words, models, and expanded form to show numbers in different ways.

Here are three ways to show 231.

Use models.

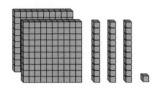

Write the number of hundreds, tens, and ones.

2 hundreds 3 tens 1 one

Show the number with addition.

200 + 30 + 1

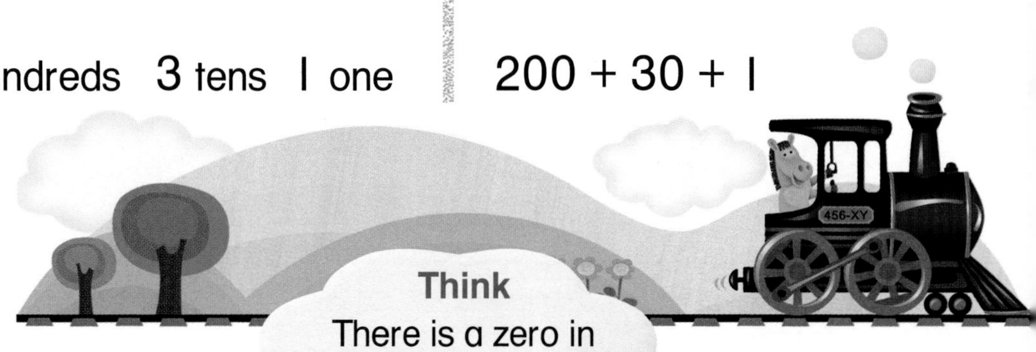

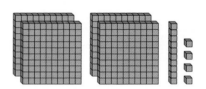

Guided Practice

Think
There is a zero in the tens place because there are no tens.

Circle another way to show the number.

1. 302

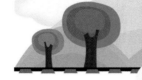

3 hundreds 0 tens 2 ones

2. 415

400 + 10 + 5

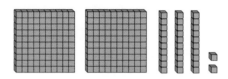

3. 150

5 hundreds 1 ten 3 ones

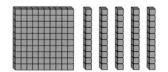

Draw or write to show the number another way.

4. 217

5. 326

TEST TIPS **Explain Your Thinking** How could you show 555 with the least number of hundreds, tens, and ones blocks?

Remember
Look for the same number of
hundreds, tens, and ones.

Circle another way to show the number.

1. 442 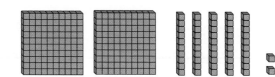 (400 + 40 + 2)

2. 205   200 + 10 + 5

3. 640   600 + 40   6 hundreds 0 tens 4 ones

4. 754   700 + 50 + 4   7 hundreds 4 tens 5 ones

Draw or write to show the number another way.

5. 485   6. 509

Problem Solving ▶ Number Sense

7. Luis has 2 pages with 100 stars each.
He has 3 pages with 10 stars each.
He has one page with 6 stars.
How many stars does he have?

Draw or write to explain.

_____ stars

 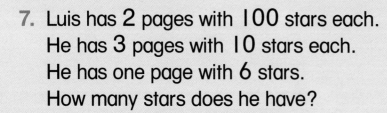 **At Home** Choose a number between 300 and 400. Ask your
child how many hundreds, tens, and ones are in the number.

Go on

Name_____

Complete the puzzle.

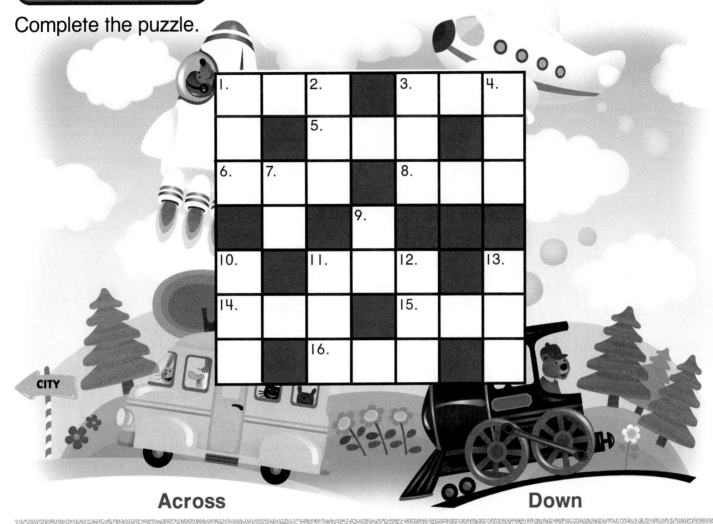

Across

1. 6 hundreds 7 tens 3 ones

3.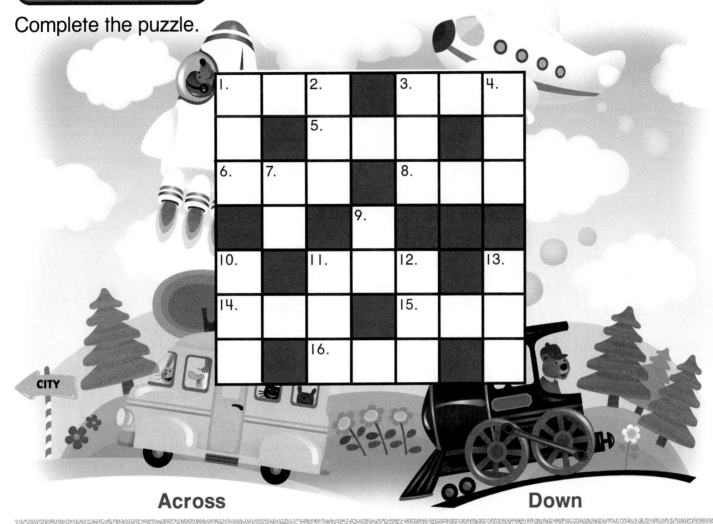

5. three hundred forty-nine

6. 3 hundreds 9 tens 3 ones

8.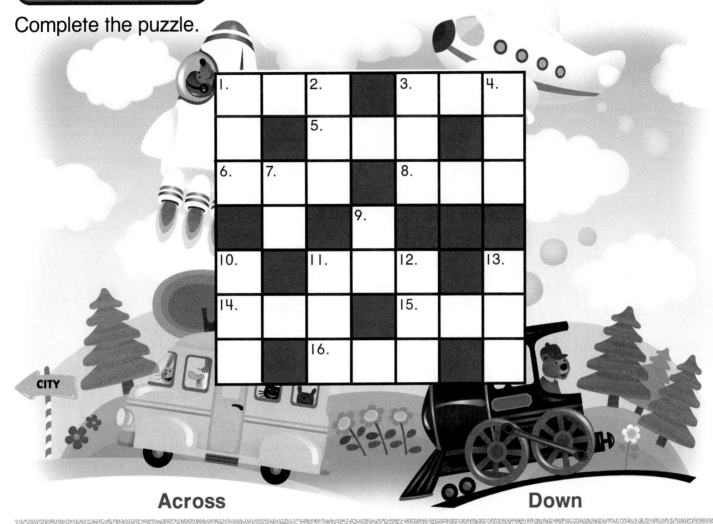

11. one hundred eight

14. 34 tens

15. 2 hundreds 3 tens 6 ones

16.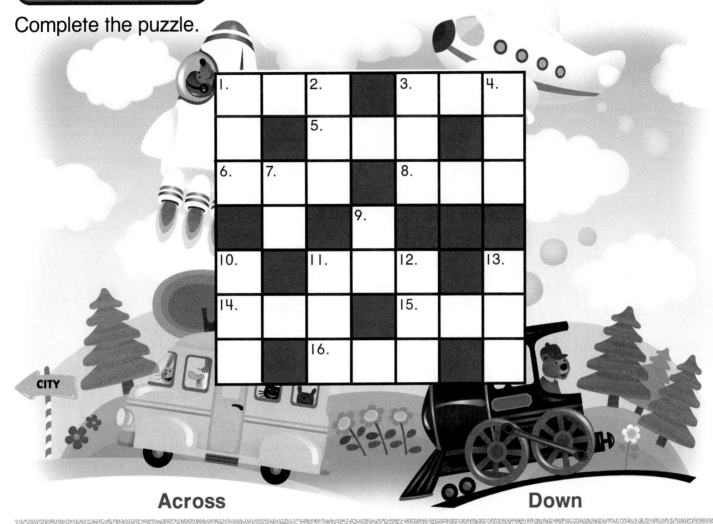

Down

1. 6 hundreds 5 tens 3 ones

2. three hundred thirty-three

3.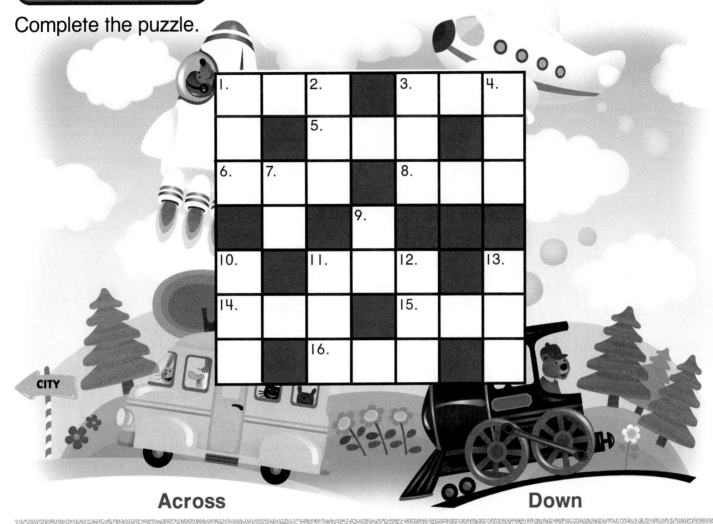

4. 2 hundreds 2 tens 6 ones

7.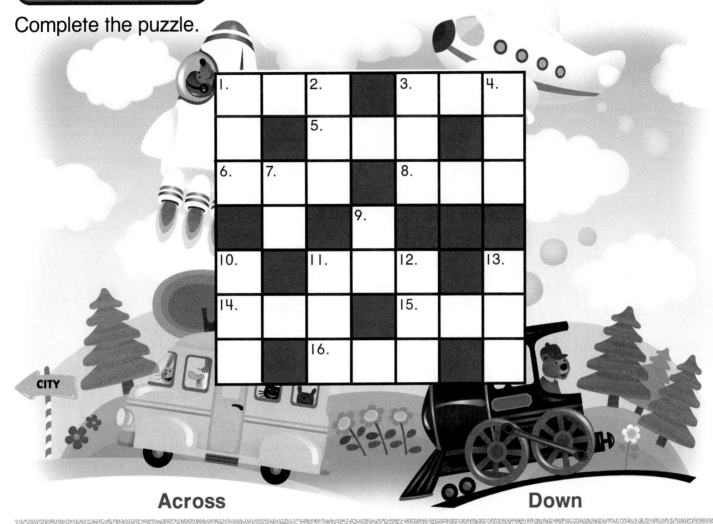

9.

10. 4 hundreds 3 tens 5 ones

11. 1 hundred 3 ones

12. 8 hundreds 2 tens 2 ones

13. 4 hundreds 6 tens 4 ones

Quick Check

Count by hundreds.
Write the missing numbers.

1. 100 200 _____ 400 500 _____ 700 _____ _____ 1,000

Count hundreds, tens, and ones.
Write the number.

2.

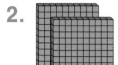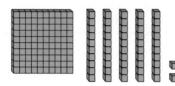

_____ three hundred fifty-two

Circle the value of the red digit.

3. 263

600   60   6

4. 948

800   80   8

5. 725

700   70   7

Write the number.

6. sixty-four _____   7. five hundred twenty-three _____

Write the number.

8. one hundred seventy-two _____

9. eight hundred six _____

Circle another way to show the number.

10. 329

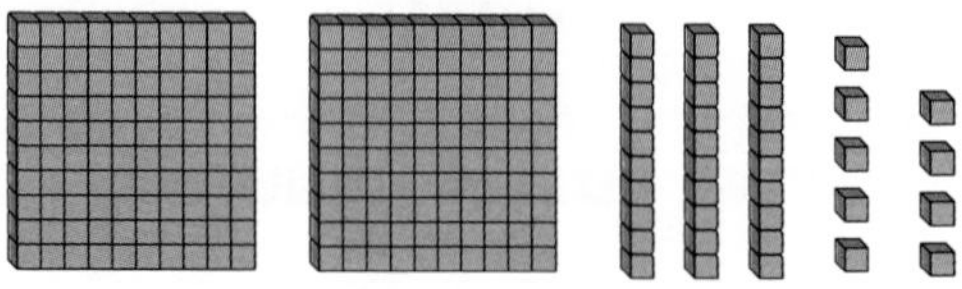

300 + 20 + 9

Before, After, Between

MathTracks 2/34
Listen and Understand

Objective
Identify three-digit numbers to determine what comes before, after, and between.

A number line can help you find a number that is just before, just after, or between two numbers.

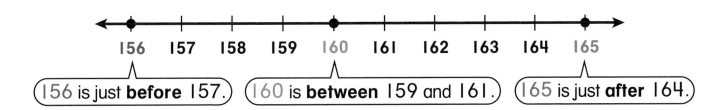

←——•——┼——┼——┼——•——┼——┼——┼——┼——•——→
156 157 158 159 160 161 162 163 164 165

(156 is just **before** 157.) (160 is **between** 159 and 161.) (165 is just **after** 164.)

Guided Practice

Use the number line.
Write the number.

←┼——┼——┼——┼——┼——┼——┼——┼——┼——┼——┼——┼——┼——┼——┼——┼→
430 431 432 433 434 435 436 437 438 439 440 441 442 443 444 445

	Before	Between	After
1.	_430_, 431	432, _433_, 434	435, _436_
2.	____, 436	437, ____, 439	440, ____
3.	____, 440	441, ____, 443	444, ____
4.	____, 438	439, ____, 441	442, ____
5.	____, 442	435, ____, 437	431, ____
6.	____, 441	430, ____, 432	437, ____

TEST TIPS **Explain Your Thinking** How would you find which number comes just before 250?

Remember
You can count to find the number.

Write the number.

	Before	Between	After
1.	560, 561	562, 563, 564	565, 566
2.	____, 566	567, ____, 569	570, ____
3.	____, 570	571, ____, 573	574, ____
4.	____, 572	565, ____, 567	561, ____
5.	____, 568	569, ____, 571	572, ____

Write the missing numbers.

6. 753 ____ ____ 756 757 758 ____ 760 ____

7. 96 97 ____ 99 ____ 101 ____ ____ 104 105

8. 595 ____ ____ ____ 599 ____ ____ 602 ____

9. ____ 993 994 ____ ____ 997 998 ____ ____

Problem Solving ▶ Reasoning

10. Kaia has cards numbered 956 through 960. She loses one of her cards. Now she has numbers 956, 957, 959, and 960.

   What card has she lost?

   Draw or write to explain.

   ____

At Home Find a three-digit number in the newspaper. Ask your child to write the numbers that come just before and just after the number.

Compare 3-Digit Numbers

 MathTracks 2/35
Listen and Understand

Use symbols when you compare numbers.

Use **>** to show **greater than.**

Use **<** to show **less than.**

Use **=** to show **equal to.**

Compare 225 and 234.

First compare hundreds.
The hundreds are the same.

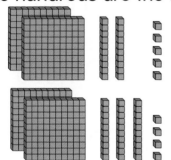

Then, compare the tens.

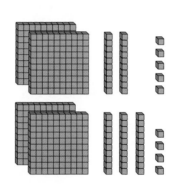

225 is less than 234.

225 < 234

Guided Practice

Compare the numbers.
Write **>**, **<**, or **=** in the ◯.

Think
The hundreds and
the tens are the same, so
I compare the ones.

1. 523 ◯ 529

2. 218 ◯ 197   3. 783 ◯ 792   4. 542 ◯ 542

5. 997 ◯ 1,000   6. 649 ◯ 621   7. 983 ◯ 973

8. 721 ◯ 689   9. 889 ◯ 882   10. 461 ◯ 468

TEST TIPS **Explain Your Thinking** Why did you need to compare the ones
in Exercise 10?

Practice

Remember
Compare the hundreds first,
then the tens, then the ones.

Compare the numbers.
Write >, <, or = in the ◯.

1. 425 ⬤< 503

2. 343 ◯ 351

3. 519 ◯ 287

4. 852 ◯ 851

5. 416 ◯ 372

6. 476 ◯ 476

7. 255 ◯ 401

8. 785 ◯ 779

9. 625 ◯ 498

10. 20 ◯ 220

11. 803 ◯ 803

12. 236 ◯ 240

13. 247 ◯ 198

14. 531 ◯ 508

15. 100 ◯ 1,000

16. 713 ◯ 713

17. 921 ◯ 912

18. 354 ◯ 352

Problem Solving ▶ Reasoning

19. Patty drove 834 miles
from San Diego to Denver.
Marco drove 844 miles
from Los Angeles to Denver.
Who drove farther?

Draw or write to explain.

_____

At Home Help your child find two numbers such as 650 and 456 in
the newspaper. Ask him or her to explain how to compare the numbers.

Name_____

Order 3-Digit Numbers

Use **place value** to order numbers from **least** to **greatest**.

Objective
Use place value to order three-digit numbers.

Vocabulary
place value
least
greatest

Order the numbers from least to greatest.

| 212 | 159 | 215 |

Compare the hundreds.

(159 is less than 212 and 215.)

Compare the tens.

(212 and 215 both have 1 ten.)

So, compare the ones.

(212 is less than 215.)

159 _____ _____

159 212 215

Guided Practice

Write the numbers in order from least to greatest.

1. 530 175 525 _____ _____ _____

Think
530 and 525 both have 5 hundreds, so I compare the tens.

2. 791 719 305 _____ _____ _____

3. 267 262 226 _____ _____ _____

Write the numbers in order from greatest to least.

4. 832 328 382 _____ _____ _____

5. 869 1,000 789 _____ _____ _____

6. 860 680 806 _____ _____ _____

TEST TIPS **Explain Your Thinking** How does knowing about place value help you order numbers?

Remember to use place value to order.

Write the numbers in order from least to greatest.

1. 199 154 291 192   _154_   _192_   _199_   _291_

2. 430 434 345 344   ___   ___   ___   ___

3. 795 800 1,000 759   ___   ___   ___   ___

4. 674 681 671 680   ___   ___   ___   ___

5. 341 314 317 374   ___   ___   ___   ___

Write the numbers in order from greatest to least.

6. 175 180 158 178   ___   ___   ___   ___

7. 922 892 927 1,000   ___   ___   ___   ___

8. 723 774 747 727   ___   ___   ___   ___

9. 509 590 501 500   ___   ___   ___   ___

Problem Solving ▶ Reasoning

10. Look at the picture. Numbers have fallen off three of the mailboxes. Put the numbers in order.

___   ___   ___

11. **Talk About It** Tell how you would put the numbers 241, 263, and 214 in order.

592 five hundred ninety-two

At Home Write 3 three-digit numbers such as 415, 411, and 381. Have your child put the numbers in order from least to greatest.

Name_____

Make a Table

You can make a table to help you solve a problem.

Toby's family takes a vacation. They drive for 5 days to get to the beach. Each day they drive 100 miles. How far do they drive?

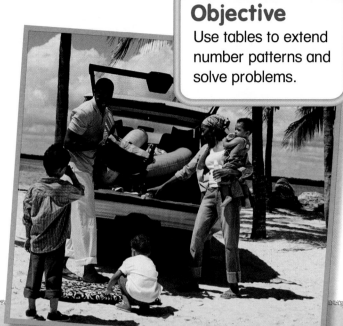

Objective
Use tables to extend number patterns and solve problems.

UNDERSTAND

What do you know?
- Toby's family drove for 5 days.
- Each day they drove 100 miles.

PLAN

You can make a table to solve.
What information do you put in your table?

number of days   number of miles

SOLVE

Make a table.
Count miles for 5 days.

Days	1	2	3	4	5
Miles	100	200	300	400	500

Toby's family drives 500 miles.

LOOK BACK

How did the table help you find the answer?
Does your answer make sense?

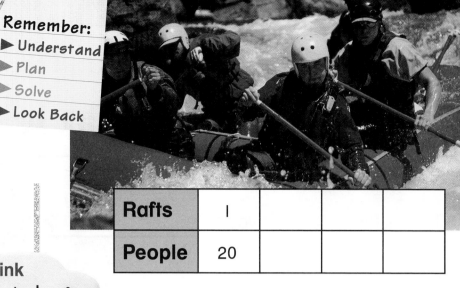

Guided Practice

Make a table to solve.

1. There are 20 people in each raft. How many people are in 4 rafts?

Think
20 people in 1 raft, 40 people in 2 rafts.

Rafts	1			
People	20			

_____ people

2. A restaurant serves 100 apples each day. How many apples does it serve in 5 days?

Think
How many days am I counting?

Days	1			
Apples	100			

_____ apples

Practice

3. There are 10 paddles in each raft. How many paddles are in 4 rafts?

Rafts	1			
Paddles	10			

_____ paddles

4. Each tent holds 6 people. How many tents are needed for 30 people?

Tents				
People				

_____ tents

Go on

Name_____

Choose a Strategy

Strategies

Guess and Check
Write a Number Sentence
Draw a Picture

Solve.

1. Tara saw 71 newts.
   36 were tan. How many
   newts were not tan?

Draw or write to explain.

newt

_____ newts

2. Hector spent 96¢ in all
   feeding the reindeer. 59¢
   was spent for crunchy
   reindeer food. He spent the
   rest of his money on apples.
   How much did he spend on
   apples?

reindeer

_____ ¢

3. There are 5 eagle nests
   along the river. There are
   2 eagles in each nest.
   How many eagles are
   along the river?

eagle

_____ eagles

4. **Multistep** There are 12
   beavers by the river. 5 swim
   away. Then 8 beavers come.
   How many beavers are by
   the river now?

beaver

_____ beavers

 At Home Ask your child to explain how he or she could make a table to solve #3.

five hundred ninety-five **595**

Listen to your teacher read the problem.
Solve.

1. Paper comes in pads of 100 sheets. Mrs. Johnson buys 5 pads. How many sheets of paper are in the 5 pads?	Show your work using pictures, numbers, or words. _____ sheets
2. The class sells muffins at the school fair. They started with 257 muffins. Which number shows how many muffins might be left after the fair?	 135 287 394

Listen to your teacher read the problem.
Choose the correct answer.

3. 429   430   431   432
         ○   ○   ○   ○

4. 375   537   735   357
         ○   ○   ○   ○

596 five hundred ninety-six

Name_____

Write the number.

	Before	Between	After
1.	_____, 521	529, _____, 531	537, _____
2.	_____, 990	914, _____, 916	919, _____

Compare the numbers.
Write >, <, or = in the ◯.

3. 428 ◯ 482   4. 302 ◯ 203   5. 787 ◯ 787

Write the numbers in order from least to greatest.

6. 682 573 473 560   _____ _____ _____ _____

7. 246 264 244 363   _____ _____ _____ _____

Write the numbers in order from greatest to least.

8. 617 716 717 616   _____ _____ _____ _____

9. 925 899 934 927   _____ _____ _____ _____

Make a table to solve.

10. A small raft holds 4 people.
    How many people are in 4 rafts?

Rafts				
People				

_____ people

Write the time.

1.

2.

4:35

3.

_____

4.

5.

6.

_____

7.

8.

9.

_____

Science Connection

A Long Trip

Scientists study how far birds can fly. The chart shows how many miles some birds can travel in one day.

Which birds can travel the most miles in one day?

_____

Birds	Distance
Barn Swallows	350 miles
Lesser Yellowlegs	316 miles
Blue-Winged Teal Ducks	125 miles

WEEKLY WR **READER** eduplace.com/kids/mw/

Chapter Review/Test

Vocabulary e • Glossary

Complete the sentence.

| hundreds |
| digit |
| least |

1. You can skip count by _____.

2. You find the value of a _____ by finding the value of its place.

3. I look at the place value of each digit to order numbers

   from _____ to greatest.

Concepts and Skills

Use Workmat 6 with ▢ , ▭ , and ▫ .

	Show this many.	Write how many.	Write the number.
4.		Hundreds / Tens / Ones	_____ four hundred sixty-five
5.		Hundreds / Tens / Ones	_____ eight hundred two

Write the number.

6. 900 + 50 + 6 _____

7. nine hundred four _____

8. 1 + 70 + 100 _____

9. three hundred seventy-six _____

10. 3 + 400 _____

11. six hundred forty-five _____

Circle another way to show the number.

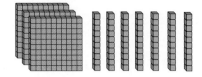

12. 307   300 + 7

13. 168   1 hundred 8 tens 6 ones   100 + 60 + 8

Write the number.

Before	Between	After
14. _____ 566	534 _____ 536	599 _____

Compare the numbers.
Write >, <, or = in the ◯.

15. 302 ◯ 305   16. 967 ◯ 697   17. 455 ◯ 455

Write the numbers from least to greatest.

18. 109   110   106   _____ _____ _____

19. 990   1,000   929   _____ _____ _____

Problem Solving

Complete the table to solve.

20. Brian's farm sells 100 pumpkins a day.
How many do they sell in 5 days?

Day	1				
Pumpkins	100				

_____ pumpkins

Adding Three-Digit Numbers

INVESTIGATION

What addition stories can you tell about the balloons?

Balloon Festival	
many colors	94
yellow	86
green	32
orange	71

Balloon Race

Follow the path that shows different ways to name the number.

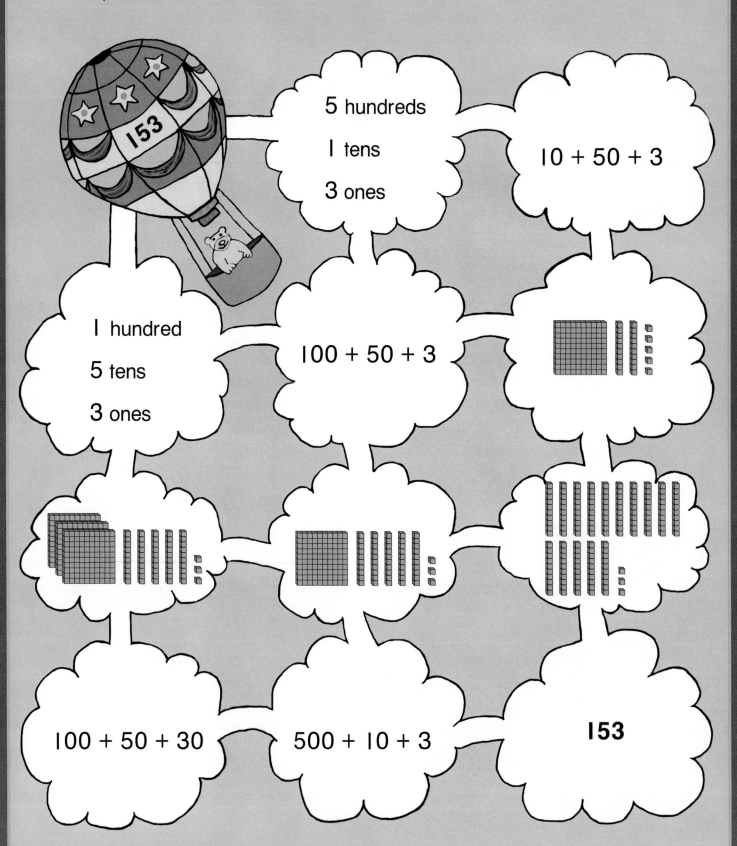

Name_____

Mental Math: Add Hundreds

Find $300 + 200$.

To add **hundreds,** think of an addition fact.

Objective
Use basic facts and mental math to add hundreds.

Vocabulary
hundreds

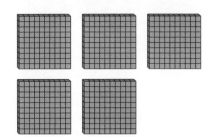

$$\begin{array}{r} 3 \text{ hundreds} \\ +2 \text{ hundreds} \\ \hline 5 \text{ hundreds} \end{array}$$

$$\begin{array}{r} 300 \\ +200 \\ \hline 500 \end{array}$$

$3 + 2$ will help you add $300 + 200$.

Guided Practice

Use the basic fact to help you add hundreds.

Think
$4 + 5 = 9$ can help me find the sum for $400 + 500$.

1. $4 + 5 =$ _____

   4 hundreds + 5 hundreds = _____ hundreds

   $400 + 500 =$ _____

2. $2 + 4 =$ _____

   2 hundreds + 4 hundreds = _____ hundreds

   $200 + 400 =$ _____

3. $\begin{array}{r} 5 \\ +2 \\ \hline \end{array}$ $\begin{array}{r} 5 \text{ hundreds} \\ + 2 \text{ hundreds} \\ \hline \text{hundreds} \end{array}$ $\begin{array}{r} 500 \\ +200 \\ \hline \end{array}$

4. $\begin{array}{r} 1 \\ +3 \\ \hline \end{array}$ $\begin{array}{r} 1 \text{ hundred} \\ + 3 \text{ hundreds} \\ \hline \text{hundreds} \end{array}$ $\begin{array}{r} 100 \\ +300 \\ \hline \end{array}$

5. $\begin{array}{r} 4 \\ +3 \\ \hline \end{array}$ $\begin{array}{r} 4 \text{ hundreds} \\ + 3 \text{ hundreds} \\ \hline \text{hundreds} \end{array}$ $\begin{array}{r} 400 \\ +300 \\ \hline \end{array}$

6. $\begin{array}{r} 2 \\ +6 \\ \hline \end{array}$ $\begin{array}{r} 2 \text{ hundreds} \\ + 6 \text{ hundreds} \\ \hline \text{hundreds} \end{array}$ $\begin{array}{r} 200 \\ +600 \\ \hline \end{array}$

TEST TIPS **Explain Your Thinking** How does $6 + 3 = 9$ help you find $600 + 300$?

Use the basic fact to help you add hundreds.

1. $1 + 2 =$ _____3_____

    1 hundred + 2 hundreds = _____3_____ hundreds

    $100 + 200 =$ _300_

2. $\begin{array}{r} 3 \\ +6 \\ \hline \end{array}$ $\begin{array}{r} 3 \text{ hundreds} \\ +6 \text{ hundreds} \\ \hline \text{hundreds} \end{array}$ $\begin{array}{r} 300 \\ +600 \\ \hline \end{array}$

3. $\begin{array}{r} 2 \\ +5 \\ \hline \end{array}$ $\begin{array}{r} 2 \text{ hundreds} \\ +5 \text{ hundreds} \\ \hline \text{hundreds} \end{array}$ $\begin{array}{r} 200 \\ +500 \\ \hline \end{array}$

4. $\begin{array}{r} 3 \\ +5 \\ \hline \end{array}$ $\begin{array}{r} 3 \text{ hundreds} \\ +5 \text{ hundreds} \\ \hline \text{hundreds} \end{array}$ $\begin{array}{r} 300 \\ +500 \\ \hline \end{array}$

5. $\begin{array}{r} 4 \\ +4 \\ \hline \end{array}$ $\begin{array}{r} 4 \text{ hundreds} \\ +4 \text{ hundreds} \\ \hline \text{hundreds} \end{array}$ $\begin{array}{r} 400 \\ +400 \\ \hline \end{array}$

Copy and Complete

6. $\begin{array}{r} 6 \\ +2 \\ \hline \end{array}$ $\begin{array}{r} 6 \text{ hundreds} \\ +\ 2 \text{ hundreds} \\ \hline \end{array}$ $\begin{array}{r} 600 \\ +\ 200 \\ \hline \end{array}$

7. $\begin{array}{r} 4 \\ +5 \\ \hline \end{array}$ $\begin{array}{r} 4 \text{ hundreds} \\ +\ 5 \text{ hundreds} \\ \hline \end{array}$ $\begin{array}{r} 400 \\ +\ 500 \\ \hline \end{array}$

8. $\begin{array}{r} 8 \\ +1 \\ \hline \end{array}$ $\begin{array}{r} 8 \text{ hundreds} \\ +\ 1 \text{ hundred} \\ \hline \end{array}$ $\begin{array}{r} 800 \\ +\ 100 \\ \hline \end{array}$

9. $\begin{array}{r} 3 \\ +2 \\ \hline \end{array}$ $\begin{array}{r} 3 \text{ hundreds} \\ +\ 2 \text{ hundreds} \\ \hline \end{array}$ $\begin{array}{r} 300 \\ +\ 200 \\ \hline \end{array}$

Problem Solving ▶ Number Sense

Draw or write to explain.

10. On Saturday, 200 hot air balloons go up in the sky. On Sunday, 400 balloons go up in the sky. How many balloons go up in the sky on both days?

_____ balloons

At Home Ask your child to tell you how knowing
3 + 2 = 5 helps him or her solve 300 + 200.

Regroup Ones

 MathTracks 2/36
Listen and Understand

Find 227 + 146.

Objective
Find the sum of two three-digit numbers, regrouping ones.

Vocabulary
regroup

Step 1

Show 227 and 146.
Add the ones. **Regroup** 10 ones as 1 ten.

Workmat 6		
Hundreds	**Tens**	**Ones**

H	T	O
☐	☐	☐
2	2	7
+ 1	4	6
		3

Step 2

Add the tens.

Workmat 6		
Hundreds	**Tens**	**Ones**

H	T	O
☐	1	☐
2	2	7
+ 1	4	6
	7	3

Step 3

Add the hundreds.

Workmat 6		
Hundreds	**Tens**	**Ones**

H	T	O
☐	1	☐
2	2	7
+ 1	4	6
3	7	3

Guided Practice

Use Workmat 6 and place value blocks. Add.

1.

H	T	O
	☐	
3	6	7
+ 2	1	8

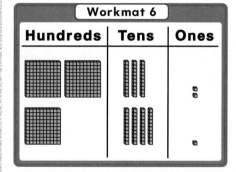
Think
7 + 8 = 15. I need to regroup 15 ones as 1 ten and 5 ones.

2.

H	T	O
	☐	
8	6	6
+		8

TEST TIPS **Explain Your Thinking** How does knowing that 15 ones is the same as 1 ten and 5 ones help you add?

Remember,
if there are 10 or more
ones, regroup 10 ones
as 1 ten.

Use Workmat 6 and place value blocks. Add.

1. 617
  + 45
  ___
  662

2. 143
  +524

3. 358
  +526

4. 318
  + 35

5. 123
  +359

6. 237
  +428

7. 468
  + 7

8. 763
  +142

9. 305
  +327

10. 223
  +619

11. 570
  + 29

Copy and Complete

12. 189
  + 307

13. 848
  + 38

14. 427
  + 119

15. 325
  + 426

16. 567
  + 226

Problem Solving ▶ Reasoning

17. **Multistep** Liz has 2 books of 100 stamps
with 6 left over. Chelsea has 3 books of
100 stamps with 8 left over. If they put all
their stamps together, how many stamps
will there be?

Draw or write to explain.

_____ stamps

At Home Ask your child to circle the exercises on this page that
require regrouping, then explain why regrouping is necessary.

Name_____

Regroup Tens

Find 152 + 265.

Objective
Add three-digit numbers with and without regrouping.

Step 1

Show 152 and 265.
Add the ones.

Workmat 6		
Hundreds	**Tens**	**Ones**

H	T	O
	1	5	2
+	2	6	5
			7

Step 2

Add the tens. Regroup
10 tens as 1 hundred.

Workmat 6		
Hundreds	**Tens**	**Ones**

H	T	O
	1	5	2
+	2	6	5
			7

Step 3

Add the hundreds.

Workmat 6		
Hundreds	**Tens**	**Ones**

H	T	O
1	1	5	2
+	2	6	5
	1	7

Guided Practice

Use Workmat 6 and place value blocks.
Add.

1.

H	T	O
	4	6	2
+	4	6	7

Think
6 tens + 6 tens = 12 tens.
I need to regroup
the tens.

2.

H	T	O
	2	5	3
+		7	5

TEST TIPS **Explain Your Thinking** How do you know if you need to regroup?

Chapter 21 Lesson 3

six hundred seven **607**

Regroup 10 ones
to make 10.
Regroup 10 tens
to make 100.

Practice

Use Workmat 6 and place value blocks. Add.

1. 183
   +526
   709

2. 357
   + 14

3. 431
   +294

4. 325
   + 66

5. 335
   +156

6. 136
   +792

7. 936
   + 48

8. 762
   + 67

9. 624
   +159

10. 342
    +364

11. 653
    +293

12. 548
    + 71

Copy and Complete

Remember to line up the digits in the ones place.

Write the addends in vertical form. Add.

13. 19 + 459

14. 260 + 179

15. 633 + 228

16. 650 + 254

17. 362 + 29

18. 263 + 129

19. 705 + 205

20. 245 + 8

21. 337 + 318

22. 354 + 127

23. 438 + 224

24. 859 + 50

25. 95 + 712

26. 361 + 472

27. 195 + 721

608 six hundred eight

Go on ▶

Problem Solving Reasoning

Solve.

Draw or write to explain.

28. Kevin flies 247 miles from Houston to Dallas. Then he flies 448 miles from Dallas to New Orleans. How far does he fly in all?

_____ miles

29. Tara travels 131 miles by bus from Cleveland to Pittsburgh. She travels another 219 miles by car to Buffalo. How many miles does Tara travel?

_____ miles

30. Carro counted the tour groups she saw. There were two groups of 100 people, four groups of 10 people, and 5 visitors who came all alone. How many people did Carro count?

_____ people

31. Use Data Susan and Juan put their postcards together. How many do they have in all?

_____ postcards

Postcards Collected	
Susan	214
Kyle	178
Juan	146

32. Create Your Own Use data from the table to write a problem. Then solve it.

_____

_____

_____

At Home Have your child explain how he or she solved the word problems in this lesson.

Quick Check

Use a fact to help you add hundreds.

1.
```
  7        7 hundreds      700
 +2       +2 hundreds     +200
```

2.
```
  1        1 hundred       100
 +5       +5 hundreds     +500
```

Use Workmat 6 and place value blocks. Add.

3.
```
 156
+217
```

4.
```
 543
+ 29
```

5.
```
 431
+318
```

6.
```
 658
+ 51
```

7.
```
 162
+275
```

8.
```
 453
+117
```

9.
```
 564
+ 70
```

10.
```
 627
+144
```

Social Studies Connection

A Flying Feat

Two brothers named Wilbur and Orville Wright built the first plane that could fly. They made the first air flight on December 17, 1903.

On the first try, their plane flew only 120 feet. But later that day, their plane flew 852 feet.

How many feet did their plane fly in these two trips?

Draw or write to explain.

_____ feet

WEEKLY WR READER eduplace.com/kids/mw/

Name_____

Add Money

Adding money is like adding other numbers. You use **dollar signs** and **decimal points** when you add money.

Rosa buys a map and sunglasses. How much money does she spend?

Add.

$1.25 + $ .65 = ☐

Line up the decimal points when you write the addition problem. Write $ and . in the sum.

$$\begin{array}{r} \$1.25 \\ +0.65 \\ \hline \$1.90 \end{array}$$

Rosa spends $1.90.

Guided Practice

Add.

Remember to write the $ and the . in the sum.

1. $$\begin{array}{r} \$3.17 \\ +4.65 \\ \hline \end{array}$$

2. $$\begin{array}{r} \$7.65 \\ +0.92 \\ \hline \end{array}$$

3. $$\begin{array}{r} \$2.62 \\ +3.28 \\ \hline \end{array}$$

4. $$\begin{array}{r} \$4.79 \\ +2.16 \\ \hline \end{array}$$

Write the addends in vertical form. Add.

5. $5.95 + $0.63

6. $3.09 + $0.74

TEST TIPS **Explain Your Thinking** How does knowing how to find 525 + 268 help you find $5.25 + $2.68?

Remember to put a $ and .

Add.

1. $2.73
   +1.50
   $ 4.23

2. $2.52
   +0.75

3. $8.47
   +0.28

4. $5.33
   +0.38

5. $0.25
   +3.58

6. $2.04
   +0.05

7. $4.99
   +2.90

8. $4.20
   +0.80

Copy and Complete

9. $ 4.65
   + 1.07

10. $ 1.91
    + 0.92

11. $ 3.50
    + 4.35

12. $ 0.57
    + 1.26

13. $ 8.37
    + 1.45

Write the addends in vertical form.
Add.

Line up the $ and . to add.

14. $3.25 + $0.66

15. $7.21 + $1.81

16. $5.41 + $3.18

17. $6.48 + $1.28

18. $8.43 + $0.82

19. $1.29 + $0.32

Problem Solving ▷ Reasoning

Draw or write to explain.

20. Kerry spends $2.37 on a sandwich
    and $1.59 on some juice. How much
    money does Kerry spend in all?

_____

At Home Have your child explain to you how to add
money amounts using the exercises on this page.

Name _____

Guess and Check

MathTracks 2/37
Listen and Understand

Joe spends $5.40 for two different tickets. Which two tickets does he buy?

BOAT RIDES

One hour $2.45
Two hours $4.25
Child's ride $1.15

UNDERSTAND

This is what you know:
• Joe spends: $5.40.
• Tickets cost: $2.45 $4.25 $1.15
• Joe buys 2 tickets.

PLAN

Use Guess and Check.
Choose two different tickets.
Add to check if the sum is $5.40.
Continue to guess and check until you find two prices that equal the whole amount spent.

SOLVE

First Guess:
• $2.45 and $4.25

$$\begin{array}{r} \$2.45 \\ + \quad 4.25 \\ \hline \$6.70 \end{array}$$

$6.70 is too much. I need to try again.

Second Guess:
• $4.25 and $1.15

$$\begin{array}{r} \$4.25 \\ + \quad 1.15 \\ \hline \$5.40 \end{array}$$

The sum is $5.40. I am done.

Joe buys tickets for the two-hour ride and the child's ride.

LOOK BACK

Did you answer the question?
How do you know your answer makes sense?

Guided Practice

Use Guess and Check to solve.

Snacks		Drinks	
fruit cup	$2.25	juice	$1.00
pretzels	$2.10	water	$1.25
nachos	$3.00	lemonade	$1.30

1. Carlo buys one snack and one drink. He spends $3.50. What does he buy?

Think
Which snack and which drink total $3.50?

Draw or write to explain.

_____ and _____

2. Mrs. Allen spends $3.90. She buys three of the same kind of drink. Which drink does she buy?

Think
Three of which drink total $3.90?

_____

Practice

3. Martin buys two different drinks. He spends $2.25. What does he buy?

_____ and _____

4. Corey buys one snack and one drink. He spends $4.30. What does he buy?

_____ and _____

Go on

Name_____

Choose a Strategy

Solve.

1. A ferry can take 20 cars across a river. If the ferry makes 4 trips, how many cars can it carry?

Draw or write to explain.

ferry

_____ cars

2. It costs $2.25 to go one mile in a taxicab. Chen goes two miles. How much does it cost?

taxicab

_____

3. An airplane leaves New York at 2:30. It lands 2 hours later. What time does it land?

airplane

_____ : _____

4. **Multistep** A subway ride cost $1.60. Tyesha pays with a one-dollar bill and 3 quarters. What is Tyesha's change?

subway

_____ ¢

At Home Help your child find the price of a favorite food. Find out how much it would cost to buy two of the item.

Listen to your teacher read the problem.
Get the data you need from the chart.
Solve.

Menu			
Sandwiches		**Salad**	
Tuna	$3.00	Potato	$1.25
Cheese	$1.25	Macaroni	$1.50
Chicken	$2.50	3-Bean	$1.00

1. You have $3.75. You spend all of it on a sandwich and a salad. What do you buy?

Show your work using pictures, numbers, or words.

_____

_____

2. Which lunch costs more, a tuna sandwich and 3-bean salad or a chicken sandwich and potato salad?

_____

_____

Listen to your teacher read the problem.
Choose the correct answer.

3.	Tuna Sandwich	Chicken Sandwich	Potato Salad	3-Bean Salad
	○	○	○	○

4.	$4.30	$4.25	$4.00	$3.30
	○	○	○	○

Quick Check

Add.

1. $4.30
   +0.89

2. $7.26
   +2.73

3. $6.82
   +2.47

4. $5.19
   +1.38

5. $1.99
   +0.25

6. $2.67
   +1.82

Write the addends in vertical form.
Add.

7. $3.48 + $0.26

8. $6.15 + $1.50

9. $ 0.45 + $3.39

Solve.
Use Guess and Check.

10. Brittany buys two items on the
    lunch menu. She spends $3.25.
    What two items does she buy?

Lunch Menu	
Chicken Soup	$1.45
Yogurt	$0.90
Fruit Salad	$2.35
Tuna Sandwich	$1.20

    _____ and _____

Key Topic Review

Write the value of each group of coins.
Compare. Write >, <, or =.

1.  _____ ◯ _____

2. 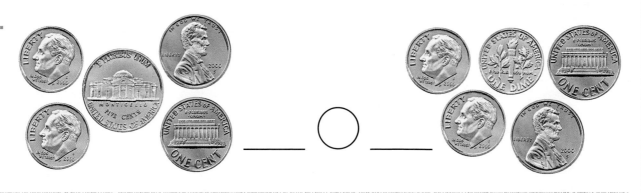 _____ ◯ _____

3. 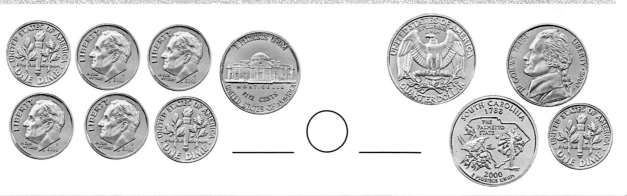 _____ ◯ _____

Math Challenge

Digit Detective

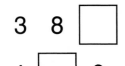

Write the missing digits.

```
  3 8 □        3 2 □        □ 5 8
+ 1 □ 9      + □ 4 7      + 4 □ 5
-------      -------      -------
  □ 9 4        8 □ 5        6 8 □
```

Chapter Review/Test

Vocabulary e • Glossary

Choose a word to answer.

1. Jacob did this exercise.
   Did he regroup ones or tens to add?

   $$\begin{array}{r} \overset{1}{2\,9\,1} \\ +1\,3\,3 \\ \hline 4\,2\,4 \end{array}$$ _____

| decimal point |
| dollar sign |
| ones |
| regroup |
| tens |

2. Write the words for each red symbol.

   $2.39   _____

   +1.15   _____

Concepts and Skills

Use the basic fact to help you add hundreds.

3. $\begin{array}{r} 1 \\ +7 \\ \hline \end{array}$ $\begin{array}{r} 1\text{ hundred} \\ +7\text{ hundreds} \\ \hline \text{hundreds} \end{array}$ $\begin{array}{r} 100 \\ +700 \\ \hline \end{array}$ 4. $\begin{array}{r} 6 \\ +3 \\ \hline \end{array}$ $\begin{array}{r} 6\text{ hundreds} \\ +3\text{ hundreds} \\ \hline \text{hundreds} \end{array}$ $\begin{array}{r} 600 \\ +300 \\ \hline \end{array}$

5. $\begin{array}{r} 2 \\ +4 \\ \hline \end{array}$ $\begin{array}{r} 2\text{ hundreds} \\ +4\text{ hundreds} \\ \hline \text{hundreds} \end{array}$ $\begin{array}{r} 200 \\ +400 \\ \hline \end{array}$ 6. $\begin{array}{r} 4 \\ +5 \\ \hline \end{array}$ $\begin{array}{r} 4\text{ hundreds} \\ +5\text{ hundreds} \\ \hline \text{hundreds} \end{array}$ $\begin{array}{r} 400 \\ +500 \\ \hline \end{array}$

7. $\begin{array}{r} 3 \\ +4 \\ \hline \end{array}$ $\begin{array}{r} 3\text{ hundreds} \\ +4\text{ hundreds} \\ \hline \text{hundreds} \end{array}$ $\begin{array}{r} 300 \\ +400 \\ \hline \end{array}$ 8. $\begin{array}{r} 5 \\ +3 \\ \hline \end{array}$ $\begin{array}{r} 5\text{ hundreds} \\ +3\text{ hundreds} \\ \hline \text{hundreds} \end{array}$ $\begin{array}{r} 500 \\ +300 \\ \hline \end{array}$

Add.

9. $\begin{array}{r} 213 \\ +149 \\ \hline \end{array}$ 10. $\begin{array}{r} 407 \\ +265 \\ \hline \end{array}$ 11. $\begin{array}{r} 819 \\ +\ \ 6 \\ \hline \end{array}$ 12. $\begin{array}{r} 372 \\ +\ 18 \\ \hline \end{array}$

Add.

| 13. | 611 +176 | 14. | 107 + 58 | 15. | 174 +333 | 16. | 473 +209 |

| 17. | 461 + 92 | 18. | 274 +195 | 19. | 382 +193 | 20. | 237 +192 |

Write the addends in vertical form.
Add.

21. $3.55 + $0.26

22. $7.55 + $0.84

23. $3.31 + $1.25

24. $3.84 + $4.24

Problem Solving

Use Guess and Check to solve.

Draw or write to explain.

25. Suki spends $6.25 on two tickets. Which two tickets did she buy?

Museum Tickets	
Adult	$4.50
Child	$2.50
Teen	$3.00
Senior	$3.75

_____

_____

Subtracting Three-Digit Numbers

CHAPTER 22

INVESTIGATION

What subtraction stories could you tell about this picture?

People Using Math

Ellen Ochoa

Has anyone ever told you to "reach for the stars"? Ellen Ochoa did.

Born in California, Ellen went to Stanford University and became an electrical engineer. She was 33 years old when she became an astronaut. Ellen has been on four flights into outer space. Two of the flights have gone to the International Space Station. At the space station, Ellen used a robotic arm to guide spacewalkers around the station.

So, the next time somebody tells you to reach for the stars, tell them you might end up there someday.

Just imagine, 480 hours equals 20 days!

Ellen spent about 480 hours in space on her first two space flights.

On her next two space flights she was in space for about 498 hours.

How many hours was Ellen in space on those 4 space flights?

Draw or write to explain.

about _____ hours

Mental Math: Subtract Hundreds

Think of a subtraction fact to help you subtract **hundreds.**

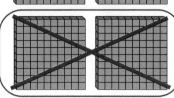

5 hundreds	500
− 2 hundreds	− 200
3 hundreds	300

$5 - 2 = 3$ is the basic fact that helps you subtract.

Guided Practice

Use the basic fact to help you subtract hundreds.

Think
I can use
$8 - 3 = 5$ to find the differences for
$800 - 300$.

1. $8 - 3 =$ _____

   8 hundreds − 3 hundreds = _____ hundreds

   $800 - 300 =$ _____

2. $6 - 4 =$ _____

   6 hundreds − 4 hundreds = _____ hundreds

   $600 - 400 =$ _____

3. $\begin{array}{r} 7 \\ -2 \\ \hline \end{array}$ 7 hundreds $\begin{array}{r} 700 \\ -200 \\ \hline \end{array}$
    _____ hundreds

4. $\begin{array}{r} 5 \\ -2 \\ \hline \end{array}$ 5 hundreds $\begin{array}{r} 500 \\ -200 \\ \hline \end{array}$
    _____ hundreds

5. $\begin{array}{r} 8 \\ -7 \\ \hline \end{array}$ 8 hundreds $\begin{array}{r} 800 \\ -700 \\ \hline \end{array}$
    _____ hundred

6. $\begin{array}{r} 9 \\ -6 \\ \hline \end{array}$ 9 hundreds $\begin{array}{r} 900 \\ -600 \\ \hline \end{array}$
    _____ hundreds

TEST TIPS **Explain Your Thinking** How does $6 - 2 = 4$ help you solve $600 - 200$?

Use mental math.

Next Galaxy
300
Light Years

Use the basic fact to help you subtract hundreds.

1. 8 − 4 = ___4___

   8 hundreds − 4 hundreds = ___4___ hundreds

   800 − 400 = __400__

2.   8   8 hundreds   800
      −5   −5 hundreds   −500
                 hundreds

3.   7   7 hundreds   700
      −3   −3 hundreds   −300
                 hundreds

4.   9   9 hundreds   900
      −1   −1 hundred   −100
                 hundreds

5.   5   5 hundreds   500
      −4   −4 hundreds   −400
                 hundred

Copy and Complete

6.   9   9 hundreds   900
      −6   −6 hundreds   −600

7.   7   7 hundreds   700
      −5   −5 hundreds   −500

Problem Solving ▶ **Mental Math**

8. The Johnsons fly 900 miles on Monday.
   They fly 600 miles on Tuesday.
   How many more miles do they fly
   on Monday than Tuesday?

Draw or write to explain.

_____ miles

At Home Ask your child to explain the patterns of ones and hundreds used during this lesson.

Regroup Tens

MathTracks 2/38
Listen and Understand

Objective
Find the difference for two three-digit numbers, regrouping tens.

Vocabulary
regroup

Find 253 – 137.

Step 1

Regroup 1 ten as 10 ones. Subtract the ones.

Workmat 6		
Hundreds	Tens	Ones

H	T	O
	4	13
2	5̸	3̸
– 1	3	7
		6

Step 2

Subtract the tens.

Workmat 6		
Hundreds	Tens	Ones

H	T	O
	4	13
2	5̸	3̸
– 1	3	7
		6

Step 3

Subtract the hundreds.

Workmat 6		
Hundreds	Tens	Ones

H	T	O
	4	13
2	5̸	3̸
– 1	3	7
1	1	6

Guided Practice

Use Workmat 6 and place value blocks. Subtract.

1.

H	T	O
	8	14
6	9̸	4̸
– 3	8	9
3	0	5

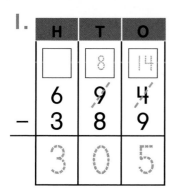
I need to regroup 9 tens and 4 ones as 8 tens and 14 ones.

2.

H	T	O
3	8	0
– 1	2	6

3.

H	T	O
2	2	6
–		9

TEST TIPS **Explain Your Thinking** How does regrouping tens and ones help you subtract?

Practice

Remember, if there are not enough ones to subtract, regroup 1 ten for 10 ones.

Use Workmat 6 and place value blocks. Subtract.

1.
H	T	O
	8	13
3	9̸	3̸
− 1	6	5
2	2	8

2.
H	T	O
1	5	9
− 1	0	7

3.
H	T	O
6	3	0
− 1	2	8

4.
H	T	O
5	6	0
− 2	2	8

5.
```
    1 9 3
  −   4 6
```

6.
```
  3 8 8
  −   7 9
```

7.
```
  5 7 2
  −   3 5
```

8.
```
  9 5 2
  − 5 1 7
```

Copy and Complete

9.
```
  432
 −329
```

10.
```
  899
 −632
```

11.
```
  751
 −218
```

12.
```
  567
 −  59
```

13.
```
  389
 −  78
```

Problem Solving ▷ Visual Thinking

14. Grasshopper and Ant are climbing a hill. The hill is 691 feet high. They have climbed 75 feet so far. How many more feet do they need to climb?

691 feet

75 feet

Draw or write to explain.

_____ feet

626 six hundred twenty-six

Regroup Hundreds

If there are not enough tens to subtract, regroup 1 hundred as 10 tens.

Objective
Find the difference of two three-digit numbers, regrouping hundreds.

Find 336 − 172.

Step 1	Step 2	Step 3
Show 336. Subtract the ones.	Regroup 1 hundred as 10 tens. Subtract the tens.	Subtract the hundreds.

Step 1

Workmat 6

Hundreds	Tens	Ones

H	T	O
3	3	6
− 1	7	2
		4

Step 2

Workmat 6

Hundreds	Tens	Ones

H	T	O
2	13	
3	3	6
− 1	7	2
	6	4

Step 3

Workmat 6

Hundreds	Tens	Ones

H	T	O
2	13	
3	3	6
− 1	7	2
1	6	4

Guided Practice

Use Workmat 6 and place-value blocks. Subtract.

1.

H	T	O
3	11	
4	1	7
− 2	6	3
1	5	3

Think
I need to regroup 4 hundreds 1 ten as 3 hundreds 11 tens.

2.

H	T	O
8	2	6
−	9	3

3.

H	T	O
3	8	2
− 1	2	6

TEST TIPS **Explain Your Thinking** When do you need to regroup 1 hundred as 10 tens?

 **Practice**

Use Workmat 6 and place-value blocks.
Subtract.

Think
Remember, if there are not enough tens to subtract, regroup 1 hundred as 10 tens.

1. ⁴¹2
    5̶2̶8̶
    −233
    _295_

2. 573
    −257

3. 943
    −471

4. 917
    −736

5. 380
    −177

6. 479
    − 99

7. 708
    − 64

8. 861
    −548

Copy and Complete

Subtract.

9. 418
    −193

10. 607
    − 26

11. 981
    −690

12. 245
    −151

13. 417
    −344

Rewrite the numbers.
Subtract.

14. 797 − 9

15. 352 − 149

16. 193 − 79

17. 368 − 49

Problem Solving ▶ Data Sense

18. How many more rooms does the Market Hotel have than the Castle Hotel?

Hotel Name	Number of Rooms
Castle Hotel	280
Sandy Hotel	560
Market Hotel	710

Draw or write to explain.

_____ rooms

628 six hundred twenty-eight

 At Home Ask your child how he or she knows if it is necessary to regroup in the subtraction problem 325 − 160.

Go on ➡

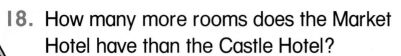

Add or Subtract to Win

2 Players

What You Need: Counters, Number Cube labeled
1, 2, 3, 1, 2, 3; Pencil and Paper

How to Play

1. Take turns tossing the number cube. Move that many spaces.

2. Follow the directions on the space. On each turn, add or subtract that number on your paper.

3. Continue until you reach the end. The player with the greater final number wins.

START with 100

Add 110

Add 206

Add 17

Subtract 50

Add 158

Subtract 32

Add 103

Add 21

Add 131

Subtract 125

Add 113

Subtract 7

END

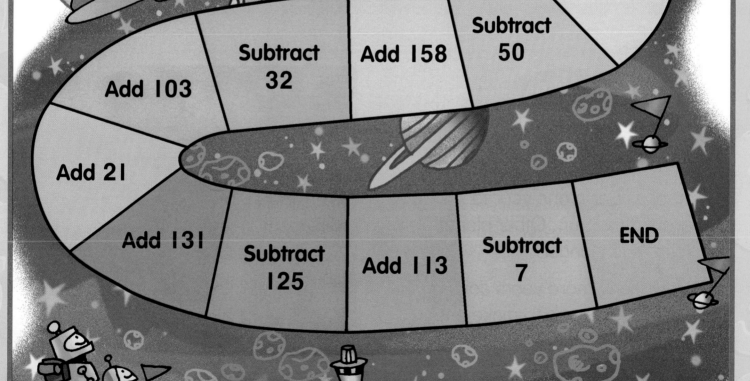

Quick Check

Use the basic fact to help you subtract hundreds.

1. 8   8 hundreds   800
   −2   −2 hundreds   −200
          _____
             hundreds

2. 9   9 hundreds   900
   −5   −5 hundreds   −500
          _____
             hundreds

Use Workmat 6 and place value blocks.
Subtract.

3.   264
   − 135

4.   489
   − 53

5.   673
   − 57

6.   745
   −   8

7.   718
   − 264

8.   829
   − 445

9.   438
   − 76

10.   807
    − 367

Connection

Orbits Around the Sun

It takes Earth one year to travel around the Sun. Other planets take much longer.

How many more years does it take for Neptune to make one trip around the Sun than Saturn?

_____ years

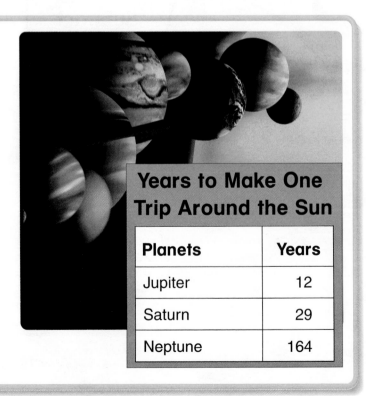

Years to Make One Trip Around the Sun

Planets	Years
Jupiter	12
Saturn	29
Neptune	164

WEEKLY WR **READER** eduplace.com/kids/mw/

Check Subtraction

MathTracks 2/39
Listen and Understand

Addition can be used to check subtraction.

Step 1

Subtract.

H	T	O
	5	1
5	6	1
−2	0	6
3	5	5

Step 2

Start with the difference, 355.
Add the number subtracted, 206.

H	T	O
	1	
3	5	5
+2	0	6
5	6	1

The sum should equal the number you subtracted from.

Guided Practice

Subtract. Check by adding.

1.
```
  573
 -239
```
[ ]
+ [ ]
_____
[ ]

Think
I add 239 to the difference to see if the sum is 573.

2.
```
  539
 -146
```
[ ]
+ [ ]
_____
[ ]

3.
```
  455
 - 37
```
[ ]
+ [ ]
_____
[ ]

4.
```
  261
 -134
```
[ ]
+ [ ]
_____
[ ]

5.
```
  617
 -436
```
[ ]
+ [ ]
_____
[ ]

TEST TIPS **Explain Your Thinking** What does it mean if the sum does not equal the number you subtracted from?

Practice

Remember to add the difference to the number you subtracted.

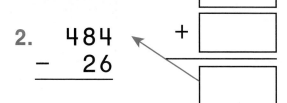

Subtract.
Check by adding.

1. 372
    −109
    263

    + 263
    ───────
       372

2. 484
    − 26

    + ☐
    ───────
       ☐

3. 652
    −161

    + ☐
    ───────
       ☐

4. 777
    −269

    + ☐
    ───────
       ☐

Copy and Complete

Find each difference.
Check by using addition.

5. 428
    −238

6. 382
    −145

7. 691
    −345

8. 596
    −189

9. 733
    −527

10. 639
     −293

11. 483
     −249

12. 932
     −704

13. 792
     − 64

14. 311
     −230

Problem Solving ▶ Reasoning

15. Julia travels 465 miles on Monday.
    She travels 218 miles on Tuesday.
    She subtracts to find the difference
    between the days and gets 257.
    Is her answer correct? Why or why not?

Draw or write to explain.

632 six hundred thirty-two

At Home Ask your child to show you how to use addition to check a subtraction problem such as 453 − 127.

Subtract Money

Subtracting money is like subtracting other numbers. You use **dollar signs** and **decimal points** when you subtract money.

Paco has $4.75. He buys a sandwich for $1.90. How much money does he have left?

Subtract.

$4.75 - $1.90 = ☐

$$\begin{array}{r} \overset{3\ 17}{\$\cancel{4}.\cancel{7}5} \\ -\ 1.90 \\ \hline \$2.85 \end{array}$$

Line up the decimal points when you write the subtraction problem.

Paco has $2.85 left.

Guided Practice

Subtract.

1. $$\begin{array}{r} \overset{6\ 16}{\$7.\cancel{6}5} \\ -\ .92 \\ \hline \$6.73 \end{array}$$

Think
Remember to write the $ and . in the difference.

2. $$\begin{array}{r} \$6.84 \\ -\ 1.09 \\ \hline \end{array}$$

3. $$\begin{array}{r} \$4.09 \\ -\ 2.39 \\ \hline \end{array}$$

Write the subtraction in vertical form.
Subtract.

4. $6.47 - $.37

5. $7.82 - $.74

TEST TIPS **Explain Your Thinking** How does knowing how to find $615 - 225$ help you find $6.15 - 2.25?

Subtract.

1. $6.10
   − 2.80

   $3.30

2. $4.89
   − 0.56

3. $3.56
   − 1.27

4. $7.78
   − 4.82

5. $9.95
   − 2.45

6. $3.88
   − 0.79

7. $2.89
   − 0.93

8. $4.82
   − 1.77

Copy and Complete

Write the subtraction in vertical form. Subtract.

Line up the decimal points to subtract. Write $ and . in your answer.

9. $4.08 − $0.56

10. $7.93 − $0.87

11. $5.19 − $0.67

12. $1.78 − $0.24

13. $8.46 − $2.66

14. $7.45 − $2.53

15. $5.09 − $3.90

16. $8.84 − $3.56

17. $6.34 − $1.42

Problem Solving ▶ Reasoning

18. Space ice cream costs $5.65. A rocket pen costs $2.29. How much more does the space ice cream cost?

Draw or write to explain.

At Home Ask your child to subtract $3.09 − $1.65, then check his or her answer by adding.

Choose the Operation

Objective
Choose addition or subtraction to solve problems.

Mrs. Carl drove to the National Air and Space Museum in Washington, D.C. She drove 280 miles on Friday and 145 miles on Saturday.

Add when you need to find how many there are in all.

How many miles did Mrs. Carl drive on both days?

Choose the operation.
Write + or −. Then solve.

280 ◯ 145 = _____ miles

Think
I add when I am putting numbers together.

Explain how you know you chose the correct operation.

Subtract when you need to find how many more.

How many more miles did Mrs. Carl drive on Friday than on Saturday?

Choose the operation.
Write + or −. Then solve.

280 ◯ 145 = _____ miles

Think
I subtract when I compare two numbers.

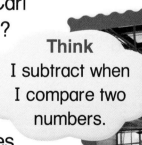

Explain how you know you chose the correct operation.

Guided Practice

Choose the operation. Write + or −. Then solve.

1. Kobe drove to Washington, D.C. He drove 410 miles on the first day and 325 miles the next day. How far did he drive?

   Think
   I need to find how far he drove in all.

   Draw or write to explain.

   410 ◯ 325 = _____ miles

2. The Air and Space Museum has 527 visitors on Friday and 473 visitors on Monday. How many more visitors are there on Friday?

   Think
   I need to compare two numbers.

   527 ◯ 473 = _____ visitors

Practice

3. Miguel counted 193 stars in the planetarium. Alana counted 146 stars. How many more stars did Miguel count?

   193 ◯ 146 = _____ stars

4. Sophie spent 170 minutes at the museum last year. She spent 220 minutes this year. How many more minutes did she spend at the museum this year?

   220 ◯ 170 = _____ minutes

Go on ▶

Name_____

Choose a Strategy

Solve.

1. There are 100 people in each tour group at the Capitol. How many people are in 4 groups?

Draw or write to explain.

Capitol

_____ people

2. At the Washington Monument, Keesha climbed 500 steps. Then she climbed 396 more steps to the top. How many steps did she climb in all?

Washington Monument

_____ steps

3. Kevin found 125 books about Mars at the Library of Congress. Ethan found 250 books about Venus. How many books did they find altogether?

Library of Congress

_____ books

4. **Multistep** Maggie arrived at the Lincoln Memorial at 1:30. She stayed for 2 hours. Then she walked 30 minutes home. What time did Maggie get home?

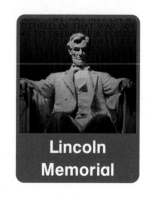
Lincoln Memorial

_____

At Home Ask your child to write a problem about traveling using the numbers 525 and 180. Then solve the problem together.

Listen to your teacher read the problem.
Solve.

1. On Saturday 439 people signed
   the visitor book. On Sunday
   326 people signed the book.
   How many more people signed
   on Saturday than Sunday?

   Show your work using pictures,
   numbers, or words.

   _____ people

2. The snack bar sold 192 bottles of
   water one hot day. It also sold
   87 glasses of lemonade. How many
   drinks did it sell that day?

   _____ drinks

Listen to your teacher read the problem.
Choose the correct answer.

3. 11   21   95   118
    ○   ○   ○   ○

4. 150 miles   500 miles   600 miles   650 miles
    ○   ○   ○   ○

638 six hundred thirty-eight

Subtract.
Check by adding.

1. 649
   −226
   + [ ]
   ─────
   [ ]

2. 618
   −234
   + [ ]
   ─────
   [ ]

3. 735
   −465
   + [ ]
   ─────
   [ ]

4. 371
   −244
   + [ ]
   ─────
   [ ]

Subtract.

5. $4.39
  −0.89

6. $7.26
  −4.73

7. $8.82
  −2.47

8. $3.09
  −1.29

9. $3.48
  −0.26

10. $6.15
   −1.50

11. $4.80
   −2.53

12. $9.85
   −1.77

Choose the operation. Write + or −.
Then solve.

13. Tony drove to Dallas. He drove
    235 miles in the morning and
    150 miles in the afternoon.
    How far did Tony drive?

Draw or write to explain.

235 ◯ 150 = _____ miles

Find the real object.
Estimate. Then measure.
Circle to show if you measured with inches or feet.

Object	Estimate	Measure
1.	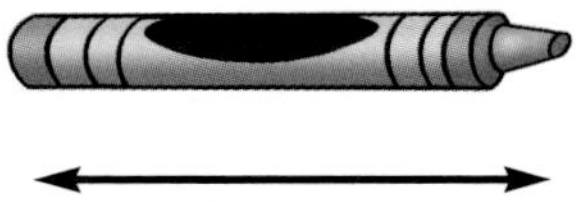 about _____ inches / feet	about _____ inches / feet
2. MY MATH	 about _____ inches / feet	about _____ inches / feet
3. 2+4=	 about _____ inches / feet	about _____ inches / feet
4.	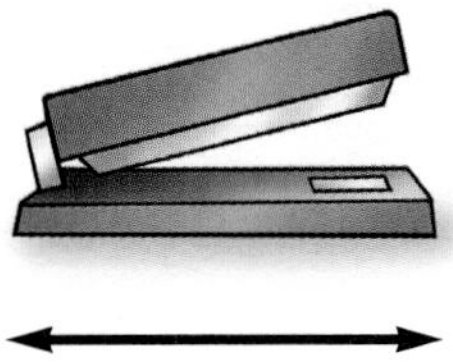 about _____ inches / feet	about _____ inches / feet

Math Challenge

Egyptian Numbers

The Egyptians used these symbols for numbers. How much is each symbol worth?

||| = 3

∩∩∩ = 30

ⓒ ⓒ ⓒ = 300

$|$ = _____   ∩ = _____   ⓒ = _____

Chapter Review/Test

Vocabulary *e • Glossary*

1. Max did this exercise. Did he regroup ones or hundreds to subtract?

$$\begin{array}{r} \overset{2\;\;15}{\cancel{3}\,\cancel{5}\,4} \\ -\;1\;6\;1 \\ \hline 1\;9\;3 \end{array}$$ _____

hundreds
ones
regroup
subtract

2. Which shows subtracting hundreds?

   8 – 2   80 – 20   800 – 200

Concepts and Skills

Use the basic fact to help you subtract hundreds.

3. 9   9 hundreds   900
   −7   −7 hundreds   −700
             hundreds

4. 6   6 hundreds   600
   −3   −3 hundreds   −300
             hundreds

5. 7   7 hundreds   700
   −6   −6 hundreds   −600
             hundred

6. 5   5 hundreds   500
   −3   −3 hundreds   −300
             hundreds

7. 4   4 hundreds   400
   −1   −1 hundred   −100
             hundreds

8. 8   8 hundreds   800
   −4   −4 hundreds   −400
             hundreds

Subtract.

9. $8.79   10. $9.32   11. $3.15   12. $5.29
   − 5.29   − 4.71   − 1.09   −0.68

Subtract.

13. 694
   −237

14. 383
   − 39

15. 520
   − 16

16. 496
   −193

17. 827
   −164

18. 605
   −274

19. 658
   −375

20. 436
   − 54

Subtract. Check by adding.

21. 917
   −792

+ ☐
────
☐

22. 385
   −127

+ ☐
────
☐

23. 615
   −232

+ ☐
────
☐

24. 490
   − 37

+ ☐
────
☐

Problem Solving

Choose the operation. Write + or − .
Then solve.

25. Sam buys a toy sailboat for
   $2.70. He pays for it with $3.00.
   How much change will he get?

Draw or write to explain.

$3.00 ◯ $2.70 = _____

Name_____

The Great Smoky Mountains

Have you ever been to the Great Smoky Mountains National Park? It is in North Carolina and Tennessee. Many visitors travel to the park each year.

Cades Cove is a popular part of the park. There are many hiking trails. There is also a beautiful campground.

Hikers on the Trail	
Friday	☺☺☺
Saturday	☺☺☺☺☺☺
Sunday	☺☺☺☺☺☺☺☺

Key: Each ☺ stands for 10 hikers.

Use the pictograph to answer the question.

1. The ranger at Cades Cove counts hikers for 3 days. How many hikers are there each day?

   Draw or write to explain.

   Friday _____

   Saturday _____

   Sunday _____

2. On Monday, 2 groups of hikers walk. Each group has 8 hikers. How many hikers are there in all?

   _____ hikers

3. On Tuesday, 20 hikers walk in groups of 5. How many groups are there?

   _____ groups

Visitors to the Great Smoky Mountains National Park can learn these facts.

- In the park, there are 238 miles of paved roads. There are also 146 miles of unpaved, or gravel, roads.

- There are more than 850 miles of hiking trails in the park.

- One famous trail is the Appalachian Trail. About 70 miles of it run through the park.

- There are 161 campsites in Cades Cove Campgrounds.

Use the park facts to solve.

Draw or write to explain.

1. How many miles of paved and unpaved roads are in the park?

_____ miles

2. Bela hikes 48 miles of the Appalachian Trail in the park. About how many more miles of the Trail is there in the park?

about _____ miles

3. One rainy night, only 107 campsites are taken. How many campsites are empty?

_____ campsites

Technology
Visit *Education Place* at
eduplace.com/kids/mw/
to learn more about this topic.

644 six hundred forty-four

Vocabulary   *e* • Glossary

Use the words in a sentence.

| equal groups |
| product |
| division sentence |

1. $12 \div 2 = 6$ is a _____.

2. _____ have the same number in each group.

3. The answer to a multiplication problem is the _____.

Concepts and Skills

Multiply.

4. $6 \times 2 =$ _____   5. $5 \times 2 =$ _____   6. $4 \times 5 =$ _____

Circle groups of 2.
Complete the division sentence.

7.

_____ ÷ _____ = _____

_____ groups

8.

_____ ÷ _____ = _____

_____ groups

Circle groups of 5.
Complete the division sentence.

9.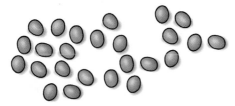

_____ ÷ _____ = _____

_____ groups

10.

_____ ÷ _____ = _____

_____ groups

Count the hundreds and tens.
Write the numbers.

11. 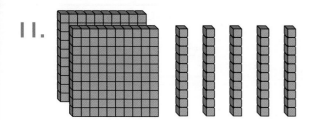   _____ hundreds _____ tens   [ ]

Write the number.

12. 700 + 40 + 8   13. 1 + 80 + 300   14. 7 + 600

_____   _____   _____

Write the numbers from least to greatest.

15. 234   241   209   _____   _____   _____

Add or subtract.

16.	248	17.	871	18.	167	19.	513	20.	490
	+ 142		− 260		− 58		+ 347		+ 106

21.	$3.42	22.	$6.78	23.	$7.41	24.	$4.48
	− 1.35		+ 2.23		− .39		− .29

Problem Solving

Draw a picture to solve.   Draw or write to explain.

25. There are 25 children on the
    basketball team. They practice in
    groups of 5. How many groups
    are there at practice?

                                            _____ groups

646 six hundred forty-six

Name ____________________

Performance Assessment

1. Draw or write 700 + 40 + 7 another way.

Show your work with pictures, numbers, or words.

____

2. Draw or write 318 to show the number another way.

Show your work with pictures, numbers, or words.

____

3. Waneta's family takes a vacation at a ranch. They ride horses every day. People ride in groups of 6. How many groups are there for 30 people?

Show your work with pictures, numbers, or words.

Group	1				
People	6				

_____ groups

Estimate Sums and Differences With Money Amounts

Round up to the nearest dollar when you estimate money amounts. Then find the sum or difference.

1. $4.80 + $2.90

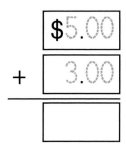

$5.00
+ 3.00

2. $6.90 − $3.80

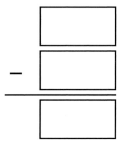

−

3. $5.60 + $2.70

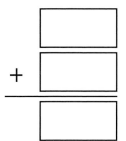

+

4. $5.90 − $3.50

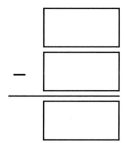

−

Round to the nearest dollar. Then add or subtract to solve.

5. Yael saves her money. She has $3.50. She gets $3.89 for her allowance. About how much money does Yael have now?

about _____

6. Carter has $10.00 for his vacation. He buys a new cap for $5.89. Then he buys a book of postcards for $1.95. About how much money does Carter have left?

Technology
Visit *Education Place* at
eduplace.com/kids/mw/
for brain teasers.

about _____

Technology Time

Calculator Broken Keys

Lee wants to show 57 on his calculator.
The 5 and 7 keys won't work. How can
Lee show 57 without using these keys?

Use a .

Here's one way.

Press: ON/C 6 0 − 3 = 57

Here's another way.

Press: ON/C 4 9 + 8 = 57

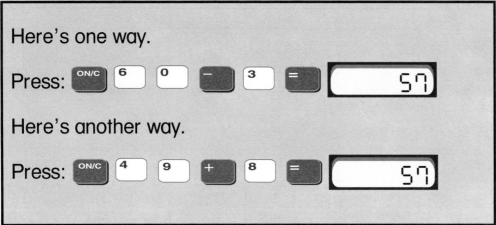

Find 2 ways to show each number. Use a calculator.
Remember, do not use the digits in the number.

Think
I can't push
the 1 or 9 button.

19 _____	27 _____
_____	_____
35 _____	371 _____
_____	_____
498 _____	246 _____
_____	_____

Cumulative Test Prep

Practice Test

Test-Taking Tips

• • • • • • • • • • • • • • • • • •

Read each problem carefully.

Check to make sure that you have answered every question.

Multiple Choice

Fill in the ○ for the correct answer.

1. About how many clips long is the ribbon?

1	2	3	4
○	○	○	○

2. Find the sum.

$$582 + 174$$

656	716	756	856
○	○	○	○

3. Multiply.

$$10 \times 6$$

60	16	6	4
○	○	○	○

4. Mark the amount of money shown.

$1.50	$1.35	$1.20	$0.35
○	○	○	○

Multiple Choice

Fill in the ○ for the correct answer.
NH means Not Here.

5. Mark the time on the clock.

9:25	5:15	4:45	NH
○	○	○	○

6. On Friday, 18 hikers climb the mountain. On Saturday, 62 hikers climb the mountain. How many more hikers climb on Saturday?

44	54	70	NH
○	○	○	○

7. Choose the shape that is a cone.

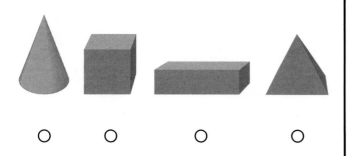

○   ○   ○   ○

Open Response

Solve.

8. Order the numbers from least to greatest.

410   441   414   401

____   ____   ____   ____

9. How are 5 + 5 and 5 × 2 the same?

_____

_____

10. Subtract.

$$466 - 238$$

Explain how you can use addition to check your subtraction.

_____

_____

_____

○○ **Test Prep on the Net**
Visit *Education Place* at
eduplace.com/kids/mw/
for more test prep practice.

Add.

Write the sum.

1.
$$5 \atop +2$$
$$6 \atop +8$$
$$1 \atop +4$$
$$10 \atop +\ 0$$
$$1 \atop +6$$
$$10 \atop +\ 7$$
$$4 \atop +2$$

2.
$$5 \atop +8$$
$$10 \atop +\ 9$$
$$1 \atop +8$$
$$3 \atop +6$$
$$6 \atop +9$$
$$3 \atop +5$$
$$8 \atop +8$$

3.
$$6 \atop +6$$
$$3 \atop +8$$
$$7 \atop +5$$
$$8 \atop +10$$
$$7 \atop +1$$
$$7 \atop +9$$
$$3 \atop +7$$

4.
$$7 \atop +0$$
$$5 \atop +5$$
$$2 \atop +1$$
$$8 \atop +4$$
$$6 \atop +7$$
$$5 \atop +9$$
$$10 \atop +\ 10$$

5.
$$9 \atop +8$$
$$3 \atop +1$$
$$6 \atop +5$$
$$9 \atop +4$$
$$0 \atop +0$$
$$8 \atop +7$$
$$10 \atop +\ 2$$

6.
$$4 \atop +6$$
$$8 \atop +2$$
$$7 \atop +4$$
$$10 \atop +\ 3$$
$$5 \atop +4$$
$$5 \atop +0$$
$$6 \atop +2$$

7.
$$7 \atop +7$$
$$0 \atop +3$$
$$4 \atop +3$$
$$3 \atop +9$$
$$2 \atop +7$$
$$9 \atop +1$$
$$3 \atop +2$$

Subtract.
Write the difference.

1. $\begin{array}{r} 18 \\ -\ 8 \\ \hline \end{array}$ $\begin{array}{r} 16 \\ -\ 7 \\ \hline \end{array}$ $\begin{array}{r} 18 \\ -\ 9 \\ \hline \end{array}$ $\begin{array}{r} 14 \\ -\ 6 \\ \hline \end{array}$ $\begin{array}{r} 16 \\ -10 \\ \hline \end{array}$ $\begin{array}{r} 19 \\ -10 \\ \hline \end{array}$ $\begin{array}{r} 17 \\ -\ 8 \\ \hline \end{array}$

2. $\begin{array}{r} 12 \\ -\ 8 \\ \hline \end{array}$ $\begin{array}{r} 20 \\ -10 \\ \hline \end{array}$ $\begin{array}{r} 17 \\ -\ 7 \\ \hline \end{array}$ $\begin{array}{r} 15 \\ -\ 8 \\ \hline \end{array}$ $\begin{array}{r} 16 \\ -\ 8 \\ \hline \end{array}$ $\begin{array}{r} 11 \\ -10 \\ \hline \end{array}$ $\begin{array}{r} 16 \\ -\ 6 \\ \hline \end{array}$

3. $\begin{array}{r} 19 \\ -\ 9 \\ \hline \end{array}$ $\begin{array}{r} 16 \\ -\ 9 \\ \hline \end{array}$ $\begin{array}{r} 11 \\ -\ 1 \\ \hline \end{array}$ $\begin{array}{r} 17 \\ -\ 9 \\ \hline \end{array}$ $\begin{array}{r} 13 \\ -\ 3 \\ \hline \end{array}$ $\begin{array}{r} 18 \\ -10 \\ \hline \end{array}$ $\begin{array}{r} 13 \\ -\ 8 \\ \hline \end{array}$

4. $\begin{array}{r} 16 \\ -10 \\ \hline \end{array}$ $\begin{array}{r} 12 \\ -\ 5 \\ \hline \end{array}$ $\begin{array}{r} 14 \\ -\ 5 \\ \hline \end{array}$ $\begin{array}{r} 17 \\ -\ 7 \\ \hline \end{array}$ $\begin{array}{r} 15 \\ -\ 9 \\ \hline \end{array}$ $\begin{array}{r} 17 \\ -10 \\ \hline \end{array}$ $\begin{array}{r} 13 \\ -\ 7 \\ \hline \end{array}$

5. $\begin{array}{r} 16 \\ -\ 8 \\ \hline \end{array}$ $\begin{array}{r} 19 \\ -10 \\ \hline \end{array}$ $\begin{array}{r} 16 \\ -\ 9 \\ \hline \end{array}$ $\begin{array}{r} 6 \\ -\ 6 \\ \hline \end{array}$ $\begin{array}{r} 18 \\ -\ 8 \\ \hline \end{array}$ $\begin{array}{r} 14 \\ -10 \\ \hline \end{array}$ $\begin{array}{r} 16 \\ -\ 7 \\ \hline \end{array}$

6. $\begin{array}{r} 18 \\ -\ 9 \\ \hline \end{array}$ $\begin{array}{r} 17 \\ -10 \\ \hline \end{array}$ $\begin{array}{r} 15 \\ -10 \\ \hline \end{array}$ $\begin{array}{r} 16 \\ -\ 6 \\ \hline \end{array}$ $\begin{array}{r} 10 \\ -7 \\ \hline \end{array}$ $\begin{array}{r} 20 \\ -10 \\ \hline \end{array}$ $\begin{array}{r} 10 \\ -\ 2 \\ \hline \end{array}$

7. $\begin{array}{r} 17 \\ -\ 9 \\ \hline \end{array}$ $\begin{array}{r} 18 \\ -10 \\ \hline \end{array}$ $\begin{array}{r} 9 \\ -3 \\ \hline \end{array}$ $\begin{array}{r} 19 \\ -\ 9 \\ \hline \end{array}$ $\begin{array}{r} 5 \\ -0 \\ \hline \end{array}$ $\begin{array}{r} 13 \\ -\ 4 \\ \hline \end{array}$ $\begin{array}{r} 17 \\ -\ 8 \\ \hline \end{array}$

Name _____

Add.
Write the sum.

1. $\begin{array}{r} 13 \\ -\ 6 \\ \hline \end{array}$ $\begin{array}{r} 10 \\ +10 \\ \hline \end{array}$ $\begin{array}{r} 6 \\ -4 \\ \hline \end{array}$ $\begin{array}{r} 9 \\ -1 \\ \hline \end{array}$ $\begin{array}{r} 11 \\ -\ 5 \\ \hline \end{array}$ $\begin{array}{r} 8 \\ +6 \\ \hline \end{array}$ $\begin{array}{r} 15 \\ -\ 8 \\ \hline \end{array}$

2. $\begin{array}{r} 6 \\ +10 \\ \hline \end{array}$ $\begin{array}{r} 10 \\ -\ 0 \\ \hline \end{array}$ $\begin{array}{r} 9 \\ +4 \\ \hline \end{array}$ $\begin{array}{r} 17 \\ -\ 8 \\ \hline \end{array}$ $\begin{array}{r} 4 \\ +5 \\ \hline \end{array}$ $\begin{array}{r} 9 \\ +9 \\ \hline \end{array}$ $\begin{array}{r} 17 \\ +\ 7 \\ \hline \end{array}$

3. $\begin{array}{r} 15 \\ -\ 6 \\ \hline \end{array}$ $\begin{array}{r} 8 \\ -5 \\ \hline \end{array}$ $\begin{array}{r} 10 \\ +\ 7 \\ \hline \end{array}$ $\begin{array}{r} 14 \\ -\ 6 \\ \hline \end{array}$ $\begin{array}{r} 9 \\ +6 \\ \hline \end{array}$ $\begin{array}{r} 18 \\ -\ 8 \\ \hline \end{array}$ $\begin{array}{r} 1 \\ +7 \\ \hline \end{array}$

4. $\begin{array}{r} 11 \\ -\ 8 \\ \hline \end{array}$ $\begin{array}{r} 7 \\ +7 \\ \hline \end{array}$ $\begin{array}{r} 9 \\ +2 \\ \hline \end{array}$ $\begin{array}{r} 20 \\ -10 \\ \hline \end{array}$ $\begin{array}{r} 8 \\ +9 \\ \hline \end{array}$ $\begin{array}{r} 13 \\ -\ 8 \\ \hline \end{array}$ $\begin{array}{r} 12 \\ -\ 2 \\ \hline \end{array}$

5. $\begin{array}{r} 5 \\ +10 \\ \hline \end{array}$ $\begin{array}{r} 12 \\ -\ 4 \\ \hline \end{array}$ $\begin{array}{r} 2 \\ +8 \\ \hline \end{array}$ $\begin{array}{r} 10 \\ +\ 9 \\ \hline \end{array}$ $\begin{array}{r} 17 \\ -\ 9 \\ \hline \end{array}$ $\begin{array}{r} 14 \\ -\ 4 \\ \hline \end{array}$ $\begin{array}{r} 2 \\ +7 \\ \hline \end{array}$

6. $\begin{array}{r} 6 \\ +4 \\ \hline \end{array}$ $\begin{array}{r} 7 \\ +5 \\ \hline \end{array}$ $\begin{array}{r} 8 \\ +7 \\ \hline \end{array}$ $\begin{array}{r} 3 \\ +8 \\ \hline \end{array}$ $\begin{array}{r} 9 \\ +5 \\ \hline \end{array}$ $\begin{array}{r} 16 \\ -\ 8 \\ \hline \end{array}$ $\begin{array}{r} 16 \\ -10 \\ \hline \end{array}$

7. $\begin{array}{r} 10 \\ +\ 3 \\ \hline \end{array}$ $\begin{array}{r} 11 \\ -\ 4 \\ \hline \end{array}$ $\begin{array}{r} 7 \\ +6 \\ \hline \end{array}$ $\begin{array}{r} 9 \\ +7 \\ \hline \end{array}$ $\begin{array}{r} 19 \\ -\ 9 \\ \hline \end{array}$ $\begin{array}{r} 2 \\ +6 \\ \hline \end{array}$ $\begin{array}{r} 16 \\ -\ 7 \\ \hline \end{array}$

Subtract.

Write the difference.

1.
8	14	3	7	12	7	4
−6	− 7	+9	+4	− 7	+8	+6

2.
12	9	8	15	6	19	7
− 3	+8	+3	− 9	+7	−10	−3

3.
4	13	5	5	7	9	10
+8	− 4	+5	−3	+9	−5	+ 8

4.
20	8	7	7	11	3	6
−10	+5	+10	−5	−5	+7	+8

5.
18	9	6	14	17	4	8
− 9	+3	+6	−5	−8	+2	−3

6.
8	15	9	16	4	8	5
+8	−6	+10	−9	+7	−8	+7

7.
6	13	11	15	1	7	13
+3	−9	−3	− 8	+9	+2	− 5